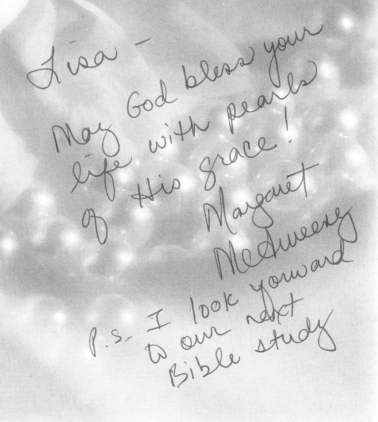

PEARL GIRLS™

encountering grit, experiencing grace

Lisa –

May God bless your
life with pearls
of His grace!

Margaret
McSweeney

P.S. I look forward
to our next
Bible study

PEARL GIRLS™

encountering grit, experiencing grace

MARGARET MCSWEENEY

General Editor

MOODY PUBLISHERS

CHICAGO

Interior Design: Julia Ryan / www.DesignByJulia.com
Cover Design: Julia Ryan / www.DesignByJulia.com
Cover Image: © 2009 JupiterImages.com
Editor: Pam Pugh

Library of Congress Cataloging-in-Publication Data

     Pearl girls : encountering grit, experiencing grace / Margaret
McSweeney, editor.
          p. cm.
     ISBN 978-0-8024-5862-9
     1. Christian women—Religious life. 2. Christian life—Anecdotes.
I. McSweeney, Margaret.

BV4527.P397 2009
242'.643—dc22

2009006119

We hope you enjoy this book from Moody Publishers. Our goal is to provide high-
quality, thought-provoking books and products that connect truth to your real needs and
challenges. For more information on other books and products written and produced from
a biblical perspective, go to www.moodypublishers.com or write to:

Moody Publishers
820 N. LaSalle Boulevard
Chicago, IL 60610

3 5 7 9 10 8 6 4

Printed in the United States of America

Dedicated in loving memory to Clarice McSweeney,
my mother-in-law, my friend, and one of the Pearl Girls,
whose life touched my heart and blessed my home.

CONTENTS

An Invitation *page 12*

An Invitation

Perhaps you have heard the story of the oyster that unexpectedly gets a piece of sand stuck inside its shell. Nacre coats this irritant and creates a pearl. Like the oyster, we encounter unexpected grit in our everyday lives: illness, loss, disappointment, pain, changes . . . and the list goes on. However, God's nacre of love and grace covers our pain and transforms us into precious pearls. PEARL GIRLS™.

Please join me as we walk along life's shore, searching for shells, scrunching our toes in the sand, and savoring sunsets. Let's become treasure seekers for the pearl of great price. Among these pages, you will read true stories about women who have unexpectedly encountered grit and experienced grace through the difficult times. You won't want to miss one of these inspiring narratives! Perhaps you will recognize your own situation or know someone else who is facing similar circumstances. My prayer is that you will find comfort and assurance of God's grace and love during life-changing moments and during the everyday challenges. You are not alone.

The unexpected grit in my life was becoming an adult orphan. Through the intense grief, however, God's grace covered my pain. He became my ultimate parent. My heavenly Father.

The first gift from my parents was my name: Margaret. I was named after my aunt Margaret who died at age twenty-two while on a student missionary trip. Margaret means "pearl." Perhaps this is what I was always supposed to do, write a book about PEARL GIRLS™.

The purpose of PEARL GIRLS™ is twofold: connecting and collaborating. As women, we are connected through our shared experiences. Together, we create an iridescent pearl necklace. With the demands and stress of everyday life, many women become secluded and disconnected from one another and from God. I hope you will take the opportunity to connect through this book. At the end, you will have the opportunity to "post a pearl" and reach out to share your own story with others. Collaborating is the other important purpose of PEARL GIRLS™. We connect to make a difference in the world. All proceeds that I receive from this book will go directly to two charities that help women and children. Information about these groups will be available at the end of the book.

Thank you, reader, for taking this journey by stepping with faith through the pages.

Margaret McSweeney

LOVE CAN WARM THE COLDEST HEART

*Ephesians 4:32: (ESV): Be kind to one another, tenderhearted,
forgiving one another, as God in Christ forgave you.*

Angels of Forgiveness

 I felt as if I had been slapped. I gaped in horror as I stared at the empty storage room and tried to comprehend my mother-in-law's words, " . . . and we even made $200!" She had sold all my worldly possessions without my permission. She was trying to be kind, but in doing so, she plowed a cavernous furrow through the garden of our friendship. I knew it would never bloom again.

Our family had just returned home after serving as missionaries for four years in Russia. We still hadn't found a place to live, and my mother-in-law wanted to help by clearing out room for us in her unfinished basement—in the space our hundred boxes of lifetime treasures once occupied. She'd sold everything from hand-knit sweaters to homemade quilts. Only a forlorn crate of John Denver records and a bag of used mittens remained.

The money she handed me from the proceeds of the sale felt like blood money. I had waited for four years to unwrap my wedding china, greet my books and knick-knacks, and slip back into my fine dresses. I couldn't believe I had put so much value on possessions, but I had, and now I was stripped.

Then I discovered she'd sold my Christmas ornaments. Every year since childhood my mother had given me a special gift at Christmas, a new and unique tree decoration that symbolized my life for that year, as well as her love for me. The box of heirloom ornaments I had so carefully packed had been sold for a dollar; my memories traded for the price of two cheeseburgers.

A ball of anger swelled in my heart. As I curled in my bed, sobbing out my grief, the ball gained momentum and became an avalanche, burying any tendril of love I had left for the mother of my husband.

Christmas loomed close and everywhere I saw beautiful, glittering Christmas trees. My tree was naked, its arms bare against the white lights. Where was the golden star with my name etched on it, or my tiny porcelain piano? How could she have done this? I felt entombed by my anger.

Sometime in January I realized I had missed the joy that came with the advent season. It couldn't penetrate my icy heart. I could barely look at my mother-in-law, despite the fact she begged my forgiveness.

"I didn't know how much this would hurt you," she said, weeping. "I was just trying to help."

I turned a stone heart to her plea. Frost laced the edges of our conversations and although I said the words, "I forgive you," my soul was an iceberg and I knew I had not.

In the past, my mother-in-law had been my greatest supporter, encouraging me, helping me pack, babysitting, and stuffing thousands of newsletters. She had cried with me, prayed for me, and tolerated me living in her home. I missed her and knew that if I wanted warmth to reenter my heart, I had to forgive her. But nothing could ease the ache of losing my memories. I avoided her and resolved to live with the pain.

When we moved away in February, I slammed the door on our relationship and didn't talk to her again.

Three days before the following Christmas, a parcel arrived at our front door, my name etched on the front. Mystified, I opened it. Then, surrounded by my family's astonished gasps, I unwrapped, one by one, a collection of angel ornaments. From bears with wings and halos to gilded crystal angels holding trumpets, I hung a choir of heavenly hosts on my tree. Finally, I sank into the sofa as my children examined the decorations, *oohing* and *aahing*.

"Who's it from?" my husband asked. I retrieved the box, dug through the tissue, and unearthed a small card. *Merry Christmas—Love, Mom* was scrawled out in my mother-in-law's script. Tears burned my eyes and, as I let them free, my icy tomb of anger began to melt. My mother-in-law was not able to retrieve the past she had so carelessly discarded, but she was hoping to build a future, our future. And it would start with these angels, proclaiming the love and forgiveness that entered our world. If God could forgive me, who stole His Son's life, certainly I could forgive my mother-in-law for stealing my . . . *stuff.*

Easter arrived and with it forgiveness finally flowered in my heart. We descended upon the in-laws for a visit and I wrapped my husband's mother in a teary embrace. I had lost the little stuffed bunnies my grandmother had knit for me, but I had gained something better—the fragrance of forgiveness, and the everlasting hope that love can warm the coldest heart.

. . . .

SUSAN MAY WARREN is the award-winning author of seventeen novels and novellas with Tyndale, Steeple Hill, and Barbour Publishing. Her first book, *Happily Ever After,* won the American Fiction Christian Writers Book of the Year in 2003, and was a 2003 Christy Award finalist. *In Sheep's Clothing,* a thriller set in Russia, was a 2006 Christy Award finalist and won the 2006 Inspirational Reader's Choice award. A former missionary to Russia, Susan May Warren now writes suspense/romance and chick lit full-time from her home in northern Minnesota.

GOD LISTENS

Jeremiah 20:9 (NIV): But if I say, "I will not mention him or speak any more in his name," his word is in my heart like a fire, a fire shut up in my bones. I am weary of holding it in; indeed, I cannot.

Cinderella

For the first time in my life, I felt like Cinderella.

But first let me back up, because the dirt of my sins was embedded in my heart. I'd made far too many mistakes as a single mom. Too numerous to list and too bad to confess even to my best girlfriend. Failed marriages and kids who needed a role model had been cast aside in favor of my own selfishness. Then God picked me up, healed my wounds, and took my hand. We began to walk together. I still slipped, but not to the gutter of despair where I'd come from. My friends commented on the change, and I didn't hesitate to tell them where my happiness and determination came from.

I understood hurt in a big way. I remember standing at my kitchen window, saying, "God, if You ever want a man in my life again, You'll have to put him at my front door wearing a T-shirt that says so." I was so reverent.

Life went on. Problems rose and fell like the tides, but with God walking beside me, I wasn't swept away, lost and alone.

My youngest son loved youth choir at church, and the piano accompanist took an interest in him. With my permission, he took my son to events and entertainment that I couldn't afford. Soon he was taking two of my other sons. My oldest son was on his own, or he'd have tagged along too. After a few months, the man began inviting me along on their excursions. At first I declined because I wanted my sons to have a relationship with just him. But he encouraged me, and I began to be a part of the group. Many nights he stopped over to help the boys with their homework, and on Sundays he picked us up for church. I enjoyed his company, and we were friends—sort of a brother/sister relationship.

One July evening, the doorbell rang. There he stood, wearing a T-shirt that said "God Listens." I felt the heat flame my neck and face. I couldn't speak. Couldn't breathe. Until that moment, I'd forgotten about the irreverent message I'd sent heavenward a few years before. "No, God. Not him. He's not the right one. Have You checked his age? He's twelve years younger than I am, and he's never been married."

Naturally, I didn't tell anyone, certain God had made a mistake.

He called on a Saturday afternoon in early September. I was stenciling the ceiling of my living room, and we chatted for a while when he cleared his throat and said, "Why don't we get married? Everyone is talking about us anyway."

I nearly fell off the ladder.

That's when I knew God hadn't made a mistake. This man wasn't the one I would have selected. We were best friends, not potential spouses. After all, I could have been his babysitter. The whole idea was ludicrous, but my own choices for husbands had failed miserably. Maybe it was time I tried God—the God of second and third and fourth and however many chances we need to get something right.

We were married in November of that year. However, the story is not over. On our wedding day, we were to be married at the church office. No fuss. No frills. Just he and I and our sons. Upon my arrival, the parking lot was full. Folks got wind of the wedding and decided to show up. At the designated time, I walked to the pastor's office where my sons waited, but the groom wasn't there. The pastor smiled and said the groom couldn't be there, but he had a letter for me.

I was devastated.

Dear God, do not let him read a "dear John" letter in front of all these people.

The letter made me cry. Every sweet word was full of how he'd come to love each one of my sons and now me. He was excited about our future and would meet me at the altar. In fact, he had a carriage ready to drive us there—wherever "there" was.

The carriage happened to be our church bus, and no one knew the destination but the pastor and the best man who video-taped my every move. When the "carriage" pulled up in front of a two-story brick house with a sign leaning against the tree that welcomed me to our new home, I wept. My soon-to-be-husband had purchased this as our new home.

For the first time in my life, I felt like Cinderella.

Did I deserve any of this? Absolutely not. The blessings were far too numerous to count, and they continue. My point? God showed me true grace and mercy with my husband. My wedding day was a gift—a taste of heaven through the love of a godly man. I can only imagine eternity.

In November 2009, we will be married sixteen years. And the blessings continue.

DIANN MILLS believes her readers should "Expect an Adventure." She is a fiction writer who combines an adventuresome spirit with unforgettable characters to create action-packed novels. Currently she has over forty books in print and has sold a million and a half copies. DiAnn is a founding board member for American Christian Fiction Writers, a member of Inspirational Writers Alive, Advanced Writers and Speakers Association, and a mentor for the Christian Writers Guild. She speaks to various groups and teaches writing workshops. DiAnn and her husband live in Houston, Texas.

THE GREATER THE DARKNESS, THE BRIGHTER CHRIST'S LIGHT WILL SHINE

*Daniel 12:3 (NRSV): Those who are wise
shall shine like the brightness of the sky, and those who lead many
to righteousness, like the stars forever and ever.*

Pushing Back the Darkness

God invites us to step into the darkness to see how bright our lamp can shine through His power. A light is never brighter than when it is shining in the darkest of nights. Leaving our lamp on the table with all the other lamps will never be as satisfying as allowing our lamp to fulfill what it was created to do—shine!

My friends Trudy and Lia came to my office to tell me about a new ministry to women in the adult entertainment industry. They invited me to join them and others in going into the nightclubs in Birmingham to encourage and minister to the exotic dancers there.

My first thoughts of this new venture of bringing Christ's light into a dark place were of the moral and social issues, what my husband might think, what my mother would say, whether my pastor would understand, how my church would respond. Yet, I could not let go of the voice within that prompted me, *If you don't go, who will? If you shouldn't go, who should?*

Although I had some reservations, I knew I had to go. I enlisted three prayer warriors who committed to pray that day, and on a Tuesday afternoon I met Trudy and Lia at a church near the club we intended to visit. We prayed intensely and then went into the club.

The bouncer met us at the door. Trudy and Lia had been to the club a few times before, so they introduced me, and the three of us went in. The music was playing as the bouncer walked us to a table away from where most of the people gathered. At first I couldn't see much of anything. My eyes focused slowly and my gaze turned toward the only spots of light in the room.

There I first saw the reason I had come: beautiful women dancing, removing the few pieces of clothing they wore in response to the tips placed in their g-strings.

Spiritual gloom sought to strangle my resolve. The darkness closed in and I had thoughts of fleeing. But that morning a dear friend had held my hands and prayed, "Lord, give her a holy cool." As I remembered her prayer, I realized that the light—the light of the world, Christ Himself—was yet available in this dark place and ready for someone through whom He could shine.

Now, nearly ten years later, this same bouncer knows us well. The darkness is as formidable as it had been at the beginning, and still tries to blind me to the light. The darkness growls, *These women don't care that you come . . . You don't have their attention when you're here . . . You can't break the cycle . . . You don't have anything to offer them . . . Remember the drugs, the alcohol, the lack of modesty, the language . . . You can't help . . . Nobody cares . . .*

Yet someone did; it was Heather who cared most recently. "I know I'm better than this," she said as I stood beside her in the dressing room. At first I was surprised to have this young woman I'd never met begin to speak as though we were longtime friends. She reached into her bag and pulled out the photos of her children and the award she had received in her college class for the highest grade. She talked about her goals to finish school.

And then she said it. "I don't want to dance anymore."

I hadn't done anything in that dressing room, except stand there praying. I hadn't even been talking with anyone. But Christ was at work. He knew where I needed to be and just who it was who was reaching out to find Him. My presence was evidence to Heather that the light of the world was a breath away. She was seeking the One who is the light that "shines in the darkness" (John 1:5). What Heather didn't know was the struggle I was going through that evening, trying to decide whether or not to keep coming. The darkness seemed so powerful that I wondered if my effort to hold out the light that is Christ was making any difference for these women. I had planned that this was going to be my last night.

Then Heather spoke. "I know I'm better than this." He was shining in the darkness. His light was pushing back the darkness. He was doing what only His light can do, and all I had to do was show up.

I would never have seen what the light who is Christ can do in the darkest of places if I had refused to go where His light shines the brightest. I've seen His light shining with hues I hadn't known were possible, breaking into lives with eternal transformation. All He asked was for someone to be there when a young woman cried out, "I know I'm better than this."

Those who are wise shall shine like the brightness of the sky, and those who lead many to righteousness, like the stars forever and ever (Daniel 12:3).

ANDREA JONES MULLINS has been publisher/director of New Hope Publishers since July 2004. She has led mission teams throughout the world, recently completed her doctor of ministry at Bakke Graduate University, and continues to minister to women who dance in the Birmingham nightclubs. She and her husband, Mike, live in Birmingham, Alabama. They have one daughter and three grandchildren.

EVERY WOMAN'S STORY NEEDS TO BE TOLD

2 Corinthians 1:3–4 (NIV): Praise be to the God and Father of our Lord Jesus Christ, the Father of compassion and the God of all comfort, who comforts us in all our troubles, so that we can comfort those in any trouble with the comfort we ourselves have received from God.

The Secret Is Out!

 The weekend began like any other. I was on summer vacation from school, and my mom and I were in the car, driving down the lane of our country home and heading into town. Our conversation on this commute would be one I would never forget.

Mom confided in me her desire to go to college and get a degree. She had talked with my stepfather about this exciting new pursuit, but he became violently angry. She was concerned by his bizarre behavior.

She looked me in the eyes. "Has he ever done anything strange around you?"

Strange? It was always strange. Frightening, horrible, disgusting, and confusing were other words I might have used. My stepfather said it was our secret and that I was special.

I felt confused. Classmates, teachers, coaches, and family friends saw me as the perfect girl, with the perfect family, and the perfect life. If that was true, then why I was living in fear and plagued with horrible nightmares? Why did I feel miserable inside? This little secret with my stepfather seemed to control me, plague me, and set out to destroy me. The thought of living with this ugly secret for the rest of my life made me want to end it all.

I began to fidget, playing with the dials on the radio, but I was really imagining what my mom would say if I told her this secret. I was unsure as to whether or not it was even wrong. Most of all, I thought it was my own fault. But I knew that if I were ever going to tell my mom, this was my chance. The next thing I knew, I was telling her something I had never told anyone, a secret my stepfather made me promise never to tell.

He had been sexually abusing me throughout my entire childhood.

My stepfather silenced me in so many ways, telling me no one would believe me and if anyone did find out about our little secret, my mom would hate me, divorce him, and I would never see her again. I believed it was my responsibility to keep our "perfect" family together; I had to protect my mom; I had to do whatever my stepdad wanted. I felt as if I had no choice. I was trapped. So, for nearly a decade I forced myself to believe that it wasn't that big of a deal. It was better if I suffered through the abuse and remained silent.

Seeing my mom's reaction, I realized that my stepfather was wrong. Mom and I prayed for direction and soon after that we left our home and reported the abuse to Children's Services.

We were in hiding, fearing for our lives. One week later we received the most shocking news: my stepfather had committed suicide.

Initially, I struggled between feeling angry and relieved. But as days and weeks passed, it got much worse. I felt alone, dirty, damaged, ashamed, and afraid of what people would think of me. I decided I would never tell my secret again.

But the pain inside only grew more painful.

The next summer, at a Christian summer camp, I did something I never thought I would be capable of doing. The final night of camp I stood in front of everyone, sharing my story, the secret I vowed to never tell again.

Later that night I was surprised when a college girl from the worship band cried as she told me her story. The next morning two high school girls shared their stories of abuse. Throughout that entire summer, I received letters from other campers: young girls, who had never shared their secret before, were now opening up to me about their painful experiences.

Little did I know when I shared that day, God would use my experiences to help so many others.

I opened my Bible and read 2 Corinthians 1:3–4: "Praise be to the God and Father of our Lord Jesus Christ, the Father of compassion and the God of all comfort, who comforts us in all our troubles, so that we can comfort those in any trouble with the comfort we ourselves have received from God."

I was beginning to understand that as horrible as my past had been, God was going to use it for good. He was comforting and healing me and He wasn't going to stop there. He wanted to use me to bring comfort and healing into the lives of others.

No matter the circumstances in your life, God wants to use them for good. You can be a comfort to others on your campus, in your community, in your circle of friends or family, in places where others are silently hurting and struggling with the same things you have endured.

I no longer live with a secret. I share my story to enable others to share theirs. I have traveled extensively for nearly a decade, speaking about sexual abuse, and I have witnessed the impact of abuse on every type of woman possible: all races, ages, classes, backgrounds, faiths. Too many of us believe we are alone in our struggles. But what we don't realize is that there are many others around us every day who are going through the same things. They need someone, they need me and you, to speak up, to provide comfort, to give hope, to encourage, and to let them know that they are not alone on their journey.

Are you carrying around a painful secret? Are you ready to receive the Lord's healing and freedom? Are you willing to use your life experiences to help others? Don't wait for someone else to break the silence. Ask God to give you strength. Find your voice. Hear someone's story. Reach out to a woman near you. Let the healing journey begin!

NICOLE BRADDOCK BROMLEY is a professional speaker and the author of *Hush: Moving from Silence to Healing After Childhood Sexual Abuse* and *Breathe: Finding Freedom to Thrive in Relationships Ater Childhood Sexual Abuse.* She is the founder and director of OneVOICE enterprises (www.onevoiceenterprises.com) and a national spokesperson on the issue of sexual abuse. Nicole lives in Columbus, Ohio, with her husband, Matthew, and son, Jude.

TRUST GOD'S UNBREAKABLE BOND
OF LOVE WITH HIS CHILDREN

Romans 8:35, 37 (NLT): Can anything ever separate us from Christ's love?
Does it mean he no longer loves us if we have trouble or calamity,
or are persecuted, or hungry, or destitute, or in danger,
or threatened with death? No, despite all these things,
overwhelming victory is ours through Christ, who loved us.

The Ties That Hold

I was numb the morning my granddaughter was born.

At that point, I couldn't really remember feeling "normal," but I knew there must have been a time. It seemed only yesterday that my life revolved around growing children and their activities, Bible studies, and volunteer work at church and in the community.

Then things began to go wrong. Two of our three children became angry and rebellious. Our younger son dropped out of school and got in trouble. My husband lost his job of twenty years. The unemployment stretched into its third year and just when our health insurance coverage stopped, our daughter got pregnant during her senior year in high school.

In the school counselor's office, I took the news calmly and courageously. I wrapped my arms around Holly and murmured something supportive. But inside I felt empty, confused, and abandoned by God. Why had He allowed so much to happen to our family? Was I to blame for everything? Why hadn't God answered my many prayers? Where was He? Where was His comfort?

Before my eyes, Holly transformed into a strong, determined young woman. She completed a mentoring program for teen moms, earning points that allowed her to purchase a crib, changing table, and other necessities. She took honors classes at school that added up to more than twenty hours of college credit, while working part-time as a waitress. Two months after graduation, Lacey was born—and transformed our family.

This beautiful child's loving spirit, sense of humor, and boundless energy touched everyone around her. And my role was something more than the average nana as Holly attended the nearby university and continued to waitress part-time. Once again I found myself rocking and burping, reading Dr. Seuss, making up songs and stories, and rolling out Play-Doh. I did my best to help nurture Lacey and support Holly, first as a single parent, and then as a wife with a husband who had joined the army.

Three years passed and I learned a new kind of heartache. Holly finished her degree early so that she and Lacey could join Brandon, now stationed at Fort Bragg. Even as I drove with them from Illinois to North Carolina, I tried to forget the fact that for the first time, I would soon be separated from my "two girls."

As I knelt in the airport, Lacey tried to ignore my explanations, but three times she called me back to her. I finally forced myself to walk away as she cried, "No, Nana! One more kiss!" I sure wasn't numb now.

Over the next few months, my husband and I treasured the phone calls from Holly, but Lacey usually couldn't be bothered to stop playing long enough to talk. I felt glad that she enjoyed being with her daddy again and exploring her new home, but a little let down that she seemed to forget me so easily after all we'd been through together.

In September Richard and I drove to North Carolina. Along the way, we wondered how long it would take Lacey to warm up to us again. Finally, we stepped out of our car and looked across a broad commons area to see Holly holding the hand of a little girl who already looked taller and older.

Time seemed to slow as we watched them walk toward us. When they stepped onto the parking lot, Lacey pressed against her mother's side. Our eyes locked; I knelt and held out my arms. Suddenly, her arms and legs wrapped around me. As I stood, she quietly laid her head down against my neck, not moving for several minutes as we both relaxed into perfect peace.

In that moment, I understood more deeply the bond of love that connects me with my granddaughter, with my children, with my family and friends. Bonds that can't be broken by distance, weakened by time, or dissolved by circumstances. Ties that hold even when relationships strain.

I also got a reminder of the strongest bond, one forged on a cross when Jesus died to make sure that nothing—not life's worst hurts or hardships, not even my own wayward emotions—can ever separate me from God's love and care.

And at last I understood just where God is when life's troubles and disappointments come. He's right in front of us, kneeling down with His arms held out, waiting for us to come and quietly lay our head down on His shoulder where we can find perfect peace.

DIANNE NEAL MATTHEWS grew up in west Tennessee and received a bachelor's degree in psychology and English from the University of Tennessee at Martin. A few years later she earned a master's of education from the University of Memphis. She and her husband, Richard, have lived in east central Illinois since 1982. They have three grown children and a gorgeous granddaughter. Dianne spends her time speaking/teaching and writing. Tyndale House published her first book in 2005, *The One Year On This Day*. *The One Year Women of the Bible* was published in September 2007. She also contributed a story to the bestselling anthology *Classic Christmas: True Stories of Holiday Cheer and Goodwill* (Adams Media, 2006). If you'd like more details, please visit her website at www.diannenealmatthews.com.

GOD WILL LEAD YOU
TO A NEW DAWN

Psalm 16:7–8 (CEV): I praise you, Lord,
for being my guide. Even in the darkest night . . .
as you stand beside me and protect me from fear.

The Darkest Night

 I turned the key. The diesel engine of my red and grey dodge pickup growled to life. The headlights cast shadows into the pine forest as I drove away from my friend's house, which was in the mountains miles away from town. My elderly cat had vanished. *God, I don't know how many more times I can say good-bye. I need to know that You care.*

The last two months had been horrific. I'd said good-bye to everything familiar—my home, my friends, my town, and most of my possessions because of a divorce. I didn't have any children, but my animals filled my heart. For safekeeping, the day I left I hugged both elderly cats, put them in kitty carriers and handed them to my friend Carol. I knew it might be months before I was settled into a home. Then I hopped into my pickup, which was pulling a horse trailer, and drove into the unknown, a forty-seven-year-old woman with three horses, one mule, and a German shepherd dog. It was a blustery January in Montana. No income. No skills to make a living. No home. And nowhere to go.

A couple of weeks later, Carol called my cell phone. "Ruby is tearing things up and wants to go outside. What should I do?"

I knew that cats usually ran away when turned loose in an unfamiliar place. But what could I do? I sighed. "Let her out. If she disappears, I'll understand."

She vanished.

A week later I had settled into a temporary home, hundreds of miles away. I drove to Carol's and picked up the one cat. I left the food and the carrier, just in case Ruby returned. But after three weeks there still wasn't a trace. I knew she probably wasn't alive. We'd been blasted with blizzards and below zero weather. The forest around Carol's was filled with coyotes and mountain lions who would love to eat kitty. Once again I drove to Carol's, my headlights piercing the night. This time I loaded an empty kitty carrier and gave Carol a hug.

As I drove away, I thought about how I had struggled to keep my thoughts focused ahead—on new beginnings. But at that moment, the weight of all my losses crushed me. I knew I'd never come back here. Ruby was gone and Carol was moving.

Suddenly my cell phone rang. I shut off the loud diesel engine. The truck lights flickered off. The blackness smothered me. It was my parents. We chatted a few minutes. I snapped the phone closed and reached for the key to start the truck. A thick cloud of grief descended on me. Grief so intense—almost like someone who was dear to me had died. Then I had a strange feeling that Ruby was watching me. That she was afraid I was going to drive off—without her—and never come back.

Could she be watching? I reached for the key. Another wave of grief washed over me.

I hopped out, into the pitch-black. "Ruby, here kitty-kitty." My feet crunched on the gravel drive.

"Ruby."

I walked ten yards and paused. "Ruuuuuuubbbbbbyyyy."

Another wave of grief slammed me. "Ruby. C'mon."

I cocked my head and listened for her body to move through the underbrush.

The next ten minutes I took one step at a time, into the black night. Then from deep within the woods, I heard it, a faint and feeble

"Mew?" Each time I called her name, she answered, but she was too scared to move.

I raced to the truck and grabbed a flashlight. I shined the beam back and forth as I climbed through the thick branches. Finally it illuminated a skeletal calico cat, crouched by a fallen tree. I clutched her to my chest. Her purr box rattled. Tears streamed down my face. God had cared. He not only protected Ruby all those weeks, but He gave me the overwhelming feeling to look for her, in the black of the night, in the woods, when there had been no trace of her.

As I stroked Ruby I thought how my life resembled this. I was groping through the darkest night. Deep in my spirit I heard, *Put your hand in Mine and I'll lead you through.*

That night was a turning point for me. The next few years were tough. But step-by-step He's led me into a life of my dreams.

REBECCA ONDOV says, "The last few years have been sprinkled with dreams and God's friendship, and I even have a new book coming out, with a tentative title of *Horse Tales from Heaven*." Rebecca lives on a ranchette nestled in the Rocky Mountains of Montana, where by day, she brokers lumber throughout the U.S. and Canada. By night she forges ahead with her mission—equipping Christians with stories that plant nuggets of faith deep in their hearts.

GOD'S GRACE GIVES STRENGTH

*2 Corinthians 12:9 (NIV): My grace is
sufficient for you, for my power
is made perfect in weakness.*

Strength in Weakness

 I first noticed the nagging pain in my soul about a year after my first miscarriage. Because a year had passed with no more pregnancies, my doctor began a battery of tests. We began our journey through the valley of infertility.

I prayed and prayed for relief from the soul pain. The physical reminder each month that I wasn't pregnant was torture enough. The soul pain became a crushing weight that I carried everywhere.

In our large Sunday school class, hardly a week passed without someone new happily announcing a pregnancy. Years passed. The same folks got up to announce their second, third, and sometimes fourth child. Baby showers were too painful so I just stopped going. I didn't want to embarrass myself or anyone else when the tears just didn't stay put in the corners of my eyes. I felt so weak, so worthless, and so forgotten.

One day, while searching the Bible for some answers, I discovered I wasn't the first person to experience such excruciating soul pain. Paul tells us of a thorn in his flesh. We're not told how that thorn manifested itself in him physically. Was Paul blind? Did he have trouble walking? That didn't matter to me. All I knew was that he prayed three times for the thorn and its pain to be removed. The answer he received was the same answer I was getting: No.

Paul's pain remained but he was not left alone or forgotten. God told him: "My grace is sufficient for you, for my power is made perfect in weakness" (2 Corinthians 12:9).

Grace. Paul was given grace to guide him through his pain. When I discovered this, we were about six years into our infertility journey. I was ready for an extra measure of grace to help me accept the "no" answer to my prayers.

With the help of prayer partners, I began to ask for grace instead of a baby. It was a strange turn in my prayer life, but one that yielded immediate results. I no longer saw pregnant women as a challenge to my sanity; I saw them as conduits of God's grace to the world. They were carrying in their swollen bellies real, live pictures of God's love. The unconditional love that each mama felt for her baby was but a tiny reflection of God's love for me. I began to feel that love anew, as though His grace had broken through the barriers I'd built around my soul. The soul pain began to subside.

One Sunday morning in church, we were singing "Shout to the Lord." I was happily singing along when the line "Nothing compares to the promise I have in You" struck me like lightning. The Holy Spirit whispered to me, *Remember that thorn, that weakness you like to go on about? It doesn't even compare to the promises you have in Me.* The promises I have in You, Lord? Right there, in that church service, promise after promise began to flood over me: the promise of eternal life, the promise of a future, the promise of unconditional love, the promise of His guidance . . . The list went on and on. The need for a child seemed so much less important as I realized everything I had, not the things I was missing.

I began to live and flourish in those promises. God began to work His power over my weaknesses. Months passed. We saw God opening doors to adoption, something closed to us before. Five weeks (not months, not years) after we met with a social worker to initiate the process, we received a call, asking us if we would adopt twin African-American boys.

The rest is history. Max and Isaac are our boys. They continue to delight us every day. Because my husband and I are Caucasian, they look nothing like us. Total strangers ask us, "Are they adopted?" Every time I'm asked that question, I feel the Spirit prompting me to answer, "Let me tell you how my weakness was made strong in God's power."

What thorn are you battling? Allow Him to use that thorn to teach you about His grace. God used the pain in my soul to produce two beautiful, lustrous, rare, and unusual black pearls. Nothing compares to the promise I have in Him.

BRENDA NEUHAUS lives in Wichita, Kansas, with Brian, her husband of seventeen years. After working in the insurance industry for ten years, she became a full-time homemaker. Brian and Brenda's twin sons Isaac and Max are now school-aged. She enjoys singing and reading, but her passion is teaching and studying the Bible, especially with women's groups. You may contact her at bjneuhaus@cox.net.

WHEN LIFE AF

Genesis 41:52 (NASB): [Jos
"God has mad

Fruit for

"What do you think God is trying to say to you?" my friend asked.

There I lay, flat on my back in bed, my knee in a special cast that was rigged with hinges that allowed the contraption I was strapped into to slowly bend my knee up and down.

A simple stroll that afternoon had ended abruptly with my being carried away in an ambulance after a driver failed to see me in the crosswalk. I found myself struggling to hold on to the front of his van, screaming for him to stop before I lost my grip and lay in the street saying my last prayers. As I cried out, "Jesus!" the driver screeched to a stop but by then the damage had been done. The tendon over my knee had been severed, making it impossible for me to get up, walk, or support myself. Three operations had followed in an attempt to repair the damage, and this was the final mile after a year of befuddling my doctor and therapist.

"I don't know," I said. "But I'm sure He'll make it clear soon." I had never cried or asked why up to this point.

I had been in this place before. Years before after moving to California in pursuit of love, and who knows what else, I found myself in a desert place. No job, no money, no love, and no idea what to do next. But that time I was angry with God. I blamed Him for tricking me. I accused

Him where He was. Little did I know that
e the entire time. Just as He had been with
d by his brothers and taken to Egypt, serving
eing thrown into jail after being wrongly accused
. . . yes the story clearly tells us that the Lord was with
rt to finish of his trial. And Joseph was able to declare to
hat what they had meant for evil God had used for good.

e to refer to my desert year in California as "the best of times,
e worst of times." It became the year that laid the foundation for
rest of my life, but it had been painful. Like the last bit of toothpaste
n the bottom of the tube, I felt that I was being squeezed until nothing
was left. I had started off with such high hopes. Finally I was going to
be with the man I loved. Finally all my dreams were going to come true.
Instead I spent a year being broken, with many friends asking if I was
sure I was in the will of God.

And yet I knew I was where I was supposed to be no matter how
uncomfortable it got. I just needed to figure out why I was in this place.
Obviously my move to California was not for the reasons I thought
it was, and as long as I clung to my first motivations, I flailed in my
discomfort. I had a picture of what my life was supposed to look like
and I couldn't see any other options . . . Ah, but when I finally let go, a
different world opened before me.

It was a time of forming new friendships, forging new alliances,
and seeing God from an entirely different point of view. And just as
quickly and painfully as it had begun, it ended, and I was back in
Chicago, back on even footing, fully restored to life as I once knew it,
but better! Yet that year in California was where I met the mentors who
gave priceless counsel as I navigated through the difficult circumstances
that ultimately grounded me in my faith.

I returned to Chicago transformed but still unfinished.

And now here I was, flat on my back, waiting to hear from God
once again.

In the silence He spoke tenderly, redirecting me back onto the path
that He had ordained for my life. This time I offered no resistance. I had
walked with Him long enough to know that when He doesn't get me

out of difficult predicaments, it's because He is trying to get something out of me. And so I let Him do His work and have His way.

In the stillness He directed me back to my initial call. "Finish the book." That was it. Years before, my mentor had encouraged me to write a book about my struggles and victories as a single woman. The moment she said it, I knew it was something I was supposed to do. I wrote my outline and the first chapter and then got distracted. Four years later I lay reading what I had written years before, understanding that now that I was grounded, I was to finish what I had started. My obedience swung open the doors to a life beyond anything I could have imagined.

Fast-forward to present. As I travel the world sharing truths from God's Word and listen to women share how my books have changed their lives, I remember life before this. The times I thought I wouldn't make it. The times that made me question where God was taking me. But in every situation I have learned that the destination is the same. He is taking me to a place of fruitfulness. Where the fruit I bear will not be for just my benefit but the feeding of multitudes. Just like Joseph! His suffering paved the way for many to be fed in the years to come.

So, all I can say is when life leads you to a difficult place, get excited. Stay focused on the journey and endure the process. Don't ask why, ask what. There's always a what. That what will always bear fruit if you let God finish what He has begun in you. And like Joseph you will be able to say that God has caused you to forget all your trouble and your previous place of suffering because the fruit you now see before you overshadows the former trial. Truly He is able to make us all fruitful in the land of our affliction and bless us with fruit that remains.

MICHELLE MCKINNEY HAMMOND. Michelle's accident was a spiritual turning point, a wake-up call to embrace her purpose and fulfill her destiny. Those bedridden months gave her time to complete her first bestselling book, *What to Do Until Love Finds You.* Michelle eventually left behind her career as an advertising art director/writer/producer for clients such as Coca Cola USA, McDonald's Corporation, Ford Motor Company, and others, to speak to audiences, encouraging people to fulfill their God-given purpose in life. She addresses real-life issues with candor and wit, answering the hard questions with sensitivity and empathy. www.michellehammond.com.

IT'S IMPOSSIBLE TO
BE SEPARATED FROM THE
PROFOUND LOVE OF GOD

*Romans 8:38–39 (THE MESSAGE): I'm absolutely
convinced that nothing—nothing living or dead,
angelic or demonic, today or tomorrow, high or low,
thinkable or unthinkable—absolutely nothing
can get between us and God's love because
of the way that Jesus our Master has embraced us.*

A Safe Embrace

 My heart beat wildly. Struggling for a breath, I felt the pillow firm against my face. Beads of sweat pooled at my neck. No amount of fighting or fidgeting would allow me to get free. I couldn't scream. I couldn't move. I couldn't breathe. Would this be the way I died? I felt his presence but was helpless and overpowered. It was no use. Suddenly I woke. Sitting up in bed, I tried desperately to gain my senses. The darkness around me felt smothering and my heart was gripped by panic. I stumbled out of bed and fumbled to find the door.

With each step, I tried convincing myself. You're okay. He's not here. You are safe now. Once in the bathroom, I hoped to be shocked into reality as the ice cold water ran over my trembling hands. Instead, I was struck with hopelessness. Hands hanging limply under the faucet, I sank to my knees on the floor. Tears rolled down my cheeks, but I wouldn't allow the sound of my sobbing to escape. It will never get better. I can't do this.

The panic attacks and flashbacks I suffered after leaving the abusive marriage were overwhelming. Once away from the horrible abuse, my mind still struggled to feel free. Even simple things like turtleneck shirts, getting overheated, or wearing constricting jewelry or clothing seemed to trigger flashbacks of getting choked, smothered, or trapped. Would I ever feel safe? Would I ever be able to stop reliving the things that happened to me?

I made my way back to bed and hoped that the covers wrapped close around me would bring comfort. Eyes shut, the images flooded my mind. The doubts consumed me, and I felt an aching deep within my heart. How will I ever be okay? Will I ever be whole again? I felt broken and afraid. I knew that leaving the situation would take great courage. And somehow, with the support of others I had mustered that. What I hadn't realized was all it would take to continue on after leaving. I felt lonely, afraid, worthless, and unlovable. Now as the images paraded through my mind, I was left to fight the demons of incidents past. Even as I attempted to clear my mind, the unthinkable images of abuse tore at me. Each thought seemed to push me further from peace and security.

"God, please help me!" I cried out in the dark. "I need You. Where are You?"

I didn't really think I'd hear His voice. Many times I had wished for His tangible presence. Why couldn't God be here to help me? Protect me? Love me?

Then, as the tears slipped slowly down my cheek, I was given the most vivid image I've ever received. It was far more vivid than the worst of nightmares, and far more comforting than my fondest dreams.

As I relived one of the horrible incidents of violence, I could see everything as it happened. He stood over me with his fist raised in anger. His face flushed with anger and motions intense with hate. Warped sounds of shouting filled the air and time seemed to move in slow motion. I could see myself huddled in a ball on the floor. My weak arms ached from blows as they shielded my face. I tried desperately to keep myself from yelling in pain and instead whimpered and gulped with each blow and kick. But the situation seemed different from the other flashbacks I had. I was oddly numb to the emotion of it all. I wasn't experiencing this from my own perspective.

And then I felt an intense comfort come over me. It was clear to me where I was. I felt Jesus' loving arms around me as we looked down on the incident unfolding. His loving arms encompassed me and protected me from every direction. His presence filled me with peace. Not one ounce of me felt fearful. In the quiet of this night, I had a new understanding. He was there all along. I had been protected in His warm, loving embrace, not just this night, but every night in the past and every night to come.

JAMI KIRKBRIDE has a passion to encourage others to make the most of every opportunity, even those painful, challenging times. She lives on a Wyoming ranch where she's inspired by her husband, Jeff, and four wonderful children. She uses her master's degree in counseling in her free-lance writing, speaking, and personality training. Jami is also a contributing author to *Laundry Tales, The Mommy Diaries,* and *When God Steps In.* For more information, visit www.JamiKirkbride.com.

SOCIETY'S WEED IS GOD'S ROSE

Jeremiah 1:5 and 29:11 (NIV): Before I formed you in the womb . . .
I set you apart . . . For I know the plans I have for you . . . to prosper you
and not to harm you, plans to give you hope and a future.

Man's Refuse, God's Jewel

"She will never amount to anything."

That was the phrase echoed over and over again by almost every teacher I had until the ninth grade. It was a phrase that I believed was true; and why not? I was born as the result of a botched abortion to a seventeen-year-old mother who did not want me.

Later, to save her marriage, she took me home to a life of horror. Her dislike for me very quickly grew into hatred and that hatred showed itself through horrendous abuse. Over the years, several more children were born into this family, a family that lived in the muck and mire of poverty, neglect, and abuse. We lived in absolute filth and everything that lifestyle brings.

I can't remember my mother ever holding me, or holding any of my siblings for that matter. But I often felt the sting of the belt, the thud of a beer stein, the stab of a knife, the burn of cigarettes, or simply hateful words crushing any sense of self-worth. In addition, my mother began taking me to see "Gramps" when I was only about three or four years of age. He was not my grandfather, but an old man who had lost his wife through death and needed someone to meet his sexual desires. I became that tool.

On the positive side, there were times my mother left me with my grandmother. It was there that I discovered books and jigsaw puzzles. My grandmother would read to me, and I soon began reading by myself. Oh, how I loved books, especially the Bobbsey Twins series. I would get lost in those tales of a happy home with parents and children enjoying time together.

On the first day of first grade, I was eager to go to school. But that excitement soon became dread as I became the "stinky kid" in class, the one no one wanted near them. That was when I first heard those hateful words: "She will never amount to anything." That became the refrain whenever I began a new grade or a new school. To ease my loneliness, I read everything I could find. I found friends in those stories; it was in them that I dreamt of loving families and friends.

Throughout my youth I was moved from foster home to foster home, from relative to relative, and back to the home of my birth. Everywhere I went, I was just that kid who did the chores or brought in extra money. Never did I find a place to belong until Marilyn entered my life.

I met Marilyn during my sixth grade year; she was someone who chose to accept me the way I was. She took me to her home to meet her parents, who were not too happy to learn that Marilyn had chosen me for a friend. But they accepted me and became the family I had hoped to have. Her mom took the time to teach me hygiene, to buy me clothes that fit, and to take me with them to church. It was there that I met my Savior and I was happy for the first time in my life.

At first, I thought that by accepting Christ, everything in my family situation would be miraculously changed; of course, it did not. When Marilyn's family moved, one year later, my refuge from the abuse was gone. I once more found myself in those same abusive situations as I continued to be passed between the foster system and my parents. I felt total abandonment. Why had God left me? Why was I left to face that so familiar life alone? I withdrew again into myself, if for nothing more than self-protection.

Then as a freshman, I was once more befriended by someone unexpected—Miss Johnson, a teacher who was a Christian. She saw my ability to learn, told me how smart I was, and helped me see that if I wanted to break free from the family pattern in which I was deeply entrenched, I needed to do well in my studies. Yes, she gave me a way out of the cycle in which I was born, but she also walked with me and shared her love and encouragement; she brought forth my love for learning; I went from barely passing my classes to earning straight A's, and continued to do so throughout high school.

There was one more hurdle to overcome during those years, though. It was passing PE when public showering was required after each class. Fortunately, the teacher, Miss Van Miller, learned of my humiliation in letting my classmates see the numerous scars on my body, and allowed me to use her private shower. She also helped me learn that God did not expect me to overcome those hurdles on my own. With her help, I again reached out to God—this time it was not to bargain for a happy family, but because He was someone who wanted me as much as I wanted Him.

As a result of these three people—Marilyn, Miss Johnson, and Miss Van Miller—I was offered the opportunity to make choices that changed the direction of my life. Rather than simply sliding into the cycle of repeating the lifestyle of my parents, I chose change. I chose to accept Jesus as my Savior, and I chose to push myself academically and socially. Life has not been easy, and my walk with Christ has had many ups and downs, but I have seen Jesus work miracles in my life.

Today, my husband and I live in a small community in Illinois, where he serves as pastor of a small country church. I teach at a local community college in western Iowa. Our children are all married, and they have given us ten wonderful grandchildren.

Oh, I may not have been seen by my early teachers as having much of a future. But they did not know what God had planned. He knew me before I was born, and He knew the plans He had for me—as a wife, mother, teacher, and public speaker.

. . . .

MARCIA LATHROP was born and raised in the Pacific Northwest and now resides in northern Illinois. She is married, has three grown sons, and ten grandchildren. She also holds bachelors' degrees in English and education, and a master's degree in education. After spending approximately twenty years in K–12 classrooms, she is currently an instructor at Clinton Community College in Clinton, Iowa, where she teaches in both the developmental and humanities departments.

GOD IS WRITING OUR LIFE STORY

1 Thessalonians 5:24 (RSV): He who calls you is faithful, and He will do it.

If We Are Willing, God Is More than Able

 Have you ever wondered about your own life story—why it seems nothing like your dreams as a young girl or why choices and circumstances led you to hard places? Do you sometimes just want God to reach down and say, "It's okay, you are definitely living the script I have for you, so hang in there"?

A few years ago on a beautiful spring day, I arrived in Boston to serve as one of the speakers for a large inspirational event. When the director informed me that the keynote speaker wanted to meet me, I couldn't help but wonder why. We met, she was delightful, and she began her story . . .

Many years ago when she was speaking in Seattle, someone asked her to visit a young mother named Inka, who was dying of liver cancer. "Cindy, I want to tell you what she and I talked about just before she died," the woman said to me. Inka was my husband's first wife.

I gulped. I wasn't sure I was ready for this. I had never met Inka, Mike's wife of ten years, but I knew her family, all of whom lived in Holland. And, of course, I had gone to court and adopted her three small children after she died. But, though I hate to admit it, I had spent my early years of marriage feeling alternately threatened by and grateful to her memory.

44

"It was hard," the speaker continued. "Inka knew she was dying and she told me so. And it was especially difficult because she was so happy to finally have a baby girl to go along with her two little boys and it saddened her to realize that she wouldn't be able to raise her children. She went on to say that she wanted Mike to marry again. But then she broke down and confessed that she was so troubled in her spirit because while she suspected Timmy and Fiona would be fine, she was worried about the future of Justin, born with mental retardation.

"Through her tears Inka cried, 'I just know there will never be a woman who can love him and help him with all his many special needs!'"

The speaker was holding my hands by now as tears ran down my cheeks. "Cindy, I prayed with her then and there, and we prayed with power, asking God to give her peace, and to provide for the husband and three precious children she would leave behind. We prayed that through God's grace, He would send a mother who could love and nurture the special needs of each of her children. And we prayed for that woman, whoever she might be, that God would give her all she needed for the great task at hand.

"After we prayed I looked at Inka's face and it was full of peace as she told me, 'I know God has answered this prayer and I can now release them all to Him.' I left the hospital room that day knowing that our precious Lord was comforting His own and providing for her in His way and His time. And I vowed I would continue to pray for the woman who would mother Mike and Inka's children. And I have."

By this time I was openly crying as she turned to me and said in the most gentle way and yet with great conviction, "Cindy, you are the answer to that prayer. I have prayed for you for eighteen years and I wanted to meet you and tell you in person of God's great moving in your life and in the lives of your family."

I am the answer to that prayer. It's one thing to know the *facts* of a situation: I married a widower and adopted his three small children who had no memory of their first mother. I knew our oldest son had terrific needs as a child, and that all the kids, while blessed with a great father, had been without a mom during three formative years before we married. It's quite another thing to learn the *heart* of a situation:

the confidences between two women and the desires and concerns of a dying young mother.

Later that day, I sat alone trying to sort out my feelings, and I thought back to the years of raising my four children (we had another daughter five years after the adoption). The early years of our marriage had been difficult and I had faltered at times wanting so desperately to be what each one needed and yet feeling so lacking. At times I thought that all I had going for me was the deep desire to be the kind of mother whose love could transform and teach and heal.

But *my* love could not do those things—only *God's love* can transform. Only *God's wisdom* can teach. And only *God's grace* can heal.

But, remarkably enough, He did it in partnership with me. I was merely the vessel, willing to be an answer to someone else's prayer, all the while finding answers to my own prayers for a loving family. "He who calls you is faithful, and He will do it" (1 Thessalonians 5:24 RSV).

LUCINDA SECREST MCDOWELL, a graduate of Gordon-Conwell Theological Seminary, is an international conference speaker and the author of seven books, including *Role of a Lifetime, Amazed by Grace, Spa for the Soul,* and *Quilts from Heaven.* Through her ministry, "Encouraging Words That Transform," Cindy enjoys creatively challenging others to live adventurously by experiencing a deeper relationship with the God of grace and mercy. She enjoys tea parties, letters on fine stationery, cozy quilts, good books, country music, bright colors, and laughing friends. Contact her through www.EncouragingWords.net.

It has now been twenty-seven years since Inka entered into glory, leaving her husband and children behind. Tim graduated from Covenant and currently works in Seattle. The "baby," Fiona, graduated from Vanderbilt, lived in Africa with the Peace Corps, and is now finishing her master's degree in London. Our fourth child, Maggie, is studying musical theatre at Belmont in Nashville. And what of that special needs son, the one whom Inka prayed for so diligently? Well, Justin is now thirty-two and has worked in the same restaurant for the past twelve years. Living in his own apartment, he is active in Bible study, volunteers with Boys Brigade, and has won several gold medals in International Special Olympics.

Does God answer prayer? Of course!

EACH LIFE EXPERIENCE, BITTER
OR SWEET, IS PART OF OUR TRAINING
AND PREPARATION FOR THE FUTURE

Philippians 4:13 (NIV): I can do all things through him who gives me strength.

A Life-Changing Phone Call

 Perhaps my name sounds familiar. I was the Verizon Airfone supervisor who spoke with Todd Beamer, a passenger on United Flight 93 on September 11, 2001. Realizing that this call was more than the representative who originally answered the phone could handle, I put the headset on and spoke to Todd. Our fifteen-minute conversation changed my life forever.

He provided details about the hijacking. As the plane began to fly erratically, I heard Todd's cries and felt physically ill and helpless. Yet, an incomprehensible peace enveloped me, and I remained calm. I knew that God was with me, and that He would give me the right words to say during this time of fear. Todd spoke about his wife and two sons. He shared that his wife was expecting a baby in January.

The bloodcurdling screams from passengers aboard Flight 93 reverberated through the headset. Part of me wanted to fling the headset and escape from this historic horror that I was hearing. However, I knew that Todd needed me to stay on the line and be there for him. He then asked me to say the Lord's Prayer with him. We prayed together.

As the plane began to turn around, he shouted, "Lisa!" He was calling for his wife, but that of course is my name, too. I assured him that I was not going anywhere and would stay on the phone as long as he needed. He told me that he and a few other passengers were going to "jump the guy with the bomb." When I asked if he was sure that's what he wanted to do, Todd responded, "Yes. I'm going to have to go out on faith, because at this point, I don't have much of a choice." His final words will be forever remembered by the American people as a motto for facing fear: "Let's roll!"

I stayed on the phone for fifteen more minutes, waiting to hear him pick it back up and speak with me again. "Todd, Todd. Are you there?" I kept calling. The other end was silent. United Flight 93 had crashed in Pennsylvania. When I finally released the call, I felt a profound grief and a sense of loss. Though I had not been physically on the plane with Todd and the other passengers, I felt as if I had been right there with them. My husband, Warren, who worked in a different area but in the same building, stayed by my side. I found great comfort having him there. Two other colleagues prayed with me.

Seven years have now passed, and a lot has changed. What a blessing to hold on to the constant love and support of my beloved husband, Warren, and our two children, Warren II and Lonye'. Through this experience, our family has grown stronger in our faith. Although I can still recall that fateful day as if it were yesterday, the raw emotions have tempered. Just like letting go of the phone was difficult, letting go of the sadness was also a challenge. Yet I remain inspired by Todd's final acts and words: "I'm going to have to go out on faith" and "Let's roll!" Facing the unknown, he leaned on his faith and acted. I pray that my willingness to take the phone call brought some words of hope and encouragement from a fellow believer. I have no doubt that one day I will meet Todd in heaven, and I will not have to let go of the phone.

LISA D. JEFFERSON is an inspirational speaker who lives in the Chicago area with her husband, Warren, and son and daughter, Warren II and Lonye'. She has received numerous awards and is currently involved with the Flight 93 National Memorial Project. She is the coauthor of *Called*, the story of her life-changing phone call. She has appeared on *Oprah*, *Larry King Live*, and many other top media outlets.

GOD'S HAND IS NEVER FAR AWAY

*Romans 8:38–39 (NIV): For I am convinced that
neither death nor life, neither angels nor demons,
neither the present nor the future, nor any powers,
neither height nor depth, nor anything else in all creation,
will be able to separate us from the love of God
that is in Christ Jesus our Lord.*

The Miracle at the Post Office

 The news was more awful than I could imagine when I pulled into the garage six years ago and found my husband home unexpectedly in the middle of the workday. He said he needed to talk with me. I followed him up the stairs and into our bedroom, with a sense of dread and fear I had never felt before. His demeanor told me something was wrong.

Seriously wrong.

He gently explained that my almost-three-year-old niece Skyler had been struck by a car backing out of the garage and killed instantly. My sister-in-law, Skyler's mother, was driving the car.

The horror of the news stunned me. I held my breath. If I didn't exhale, maybe it wouldn't be true. Maybe I had misheard. If I didn't move, maybe I could reverse what happened. But I couldn't hold my breath forever and when I exhaled, I heard a strange keening sound coming out of my body. It was the sound that grief makes when it sneaks up and pounces with no warning.

Of course my faith was shaken. Why would God let a little girl be taken in such an unimaginable way?

Looking back, I realize it was the wrong question. I would have been wiser to ask, "Are You still here, God, even in the midst of the disbelief and grief?"

I now know that He was because tiny miracles saved my faith.

There was the fact that my sister-in-law's entire extended family was able to get seats on the same airplane, in the same row, with just a few days' notice in order to get to the memorial service. And that most of my many cousins were willing and able to travel to the service, with some of them making return trips to care for my brother and his wife. And that I had a coterie of my own friends who juggled duties watching my young children so that I could do the same. And most miraculous of all was the coincidence of the clothes.

Just days before the accident, I had boxed up pants, dresses, shirts, and pajamas worn by my daughter Marissa and sent them addressed to Skyler. After returning from the memorial service, I realized with dismay that the clothes would arrive within days. I called the post office and explained my plight. Crying so hard I could hardly speak, I asked the postal employee if there was any way to intercept the package. His voice was tender as he responded. "I'm sorry, ma'am. There's no way to prevent the package from being delivered."

The timing was devastating. I called my brother and tearfully asked him to intercept the package. I didn't want to cause my sister-in-law any more grief. I worried about that package endlessly. And each day, I expected my brother to call to tell me the package had arrived. He never did.

Three weeks after sending the package, I got a letter from the post office. My mailing label had become detached. If I filled out a lost parcel form, the postal service would do its best to locate the box and deliver it. I laid my head down and cried tears of relief. A miracle had occurred in the lost parcel center of the United States Postal Service. My faith, which had withered in the days and weeks following the accident, sprouted a new, tiny shoot. This tiny miracle gave me hope that my belief could survive.

I've mailed hundreds, if not thousands, of pieces of mail over the years. What are the chances that the one piece I didn't want delivered wouldn't be? The coincidence still astounds me.

But it wasn't a coincidence after all. It was God, reaching down from heaven, to touch both a grieving aunt and a bereft mother to let them know that even in the midst of the most unimaginable pain, He cares about us and can use circumstances to show His love for us. Miracles do occur even at the post office.

MARY M. BYERS is the author of five books for women, including *The S.O.S. for PMS* and *Making Work at Home Work: Successfully Growing a Business and a Family Under One Roof.* She's also a professional speaker who specializes in leadership topics and encouraging individuals to live up to their full potential. Mary is the mother of two preteens and makes her home in central Illinois. Visit Mary online at www.marybyers.com.

GOD KNOWS THE DEPTHS
OF OUR LOSS AND WILL COMFORT US
IN OUR HEARTACHE

*Psalm 147:3 (NIV): He heals the brokenhearted
and binds up their wounds.*

The Gift

"How could I ever prepare for an absence the size of you?"
POET UNKNOWN

 My mother committed suicide when I was twenty-six. She suffered from manic depression. The whys and hows of her death don't alter the pain we suffered; they don't buffer our hearts or close the book. We've been walking this loss for twenty years and we've yet to spy the end of it. It feels so dense we can't punch our way through, so high we can't see the sun.

I've marked my grief by the milestones I pass. She wasn't there when my doctor told me I was infertile, or when I went shopping alone for our soon-to-be-adopted son. Nor was she there the day Zachary was born, or the day he took his first steps, or the day he became a brother to Tera. At each of those milestones, her absence thickened the room and dulled the light.

Every milestone hurt but one in particular had a disproportional sting. On a September afternoon a few years back, I sat on my living room floor and yanked open the first of four boxes that had just arrived from my publisher. And there it was—a book with my name on the cover. There's no explaining the thoughts and feelings that rush over you when you hold that first book in your hands. I'm not sure even a writer can put words to that moment. But even while I sat there holding that book, a shadow fell across the moment and stole a piece of my joy. My mother wasn't there to share this milestone.

I grieved anew for weeks. What would she think? What would she say? I knew of course, and yet I wanted to hear it straight from her. I thought again of the selfishness of her death, and how the ripple of that one moment has yet to strike a shore. My frustration was palpable. I couldn't remedy this lack. I couldn't take a single action that could pry the words I needed from my mother's lips.

Early one Sunday, still stinging, I went into my office to search my files. I needed a piece of colored plastic for a toddler's craft I would be teaching that morning. I had a notion that I'd kept an old college report in which I'd been asked to do a little creative writing. As an assignment for my special needs class, I had to keep a log of the daily activities of my imaginary, vision-impaired son. Digging through, I found the report, encased in a transparent blue report cover—just what I was looking for.

I smiled when I saw it. How had I remembered that? Flipping the cover open, I released the tabs, pulled the pages out and tossed them in the garbage. I didn't need the report. I didn't even know why I'd kept it all that time. But I was glad I'd kept the plastic cover.

Later that afternoon I went back to my office to find a book and noticed the garbage needed emptying—especially with the added pages I'd thrown in that morning. Walking over to pick it up, I glanced down and saw that the report had separated itself into two halves, one flopping forward and one flopping back. And right in the center, tucked down deep, I saw just the edge of a half-sheet of paper. An inexplicable nudge made me reach down into that shadowy spot and pull out the page. Holding it up, I saw familiar, lovely handwriting, and read this:

Shannon,
Dad and I really thought you did a terrific job on your story. You sure write well. Love you much,
Mom

Her words held me like a hug. I cried, and reread her note over and over. And then I found a frame for it, and placed it near my desk where I can see it easily. I can't count the times my eyes have drifted to her words. God brought me a gift—a whisper across the years, a nod of approval, a touch from a hand I long to hold.

. . . .

I will never stop missing my mother. But I've realized something odd: I know her better today than the day we buried her. I suppose that's because I'm a mother myself now, so I understand the pride she felt for us, and her gladly made sacrifices. I recognize now those times when she gave us her portion and lied about not being hungry. I understand the odd combination of love and anger and fear that filled her heart those nights she waited up to hear my key turn in the door. I know the questions she had about the future, and her place in it. I know her better, and if she were alive now, she'd be my friend.

I know my Father better, too.

SHANNON WOODWARD has written or coauthored nine nonfiction books, including *Inconceivable: Finding Peace in the Midst of Infertility* and *A Whisper in Winter: Stories of Hearing God's Voice in Every Season of Life*. She is a pastor's wife, senior editor for *The Word for Today* and Calvary Chapel Publishing, an adjunct faculty member for Imago Dei Bible Institute, and a columnist for Christian Women Online. Visit her at www.windscraps.blogspot.com or www.shannonwoodward.com.

NEVER FEAR THE BONDAGE-
BREAKING TRUTH

John 8:32 (NIV): You will know the truth, and the truth will set you free.

Half Empty/Half Full

 I had recently given birth to our third son. Jonathan was about six weeks old and slowly but surely I was learning how to divide my energy, enthusiasm, and time between the older two boys, this delightful new addition, and my husband, who was busy holding down three jobs at the time.

Being a woman of high energy and extreme enthusiasm, those two categories were not a challenge for me. Time, however, was another story. It was taking me longer than I had anticipated to adjust to the changes and time demands that came with the arrival of a third child.

The phone rang and I was pleased to discover that it was a surprise call from a dear friend of mine from graduate school.

"Have you got time to talk?" she inquired. "What's new?"

"Absolutely I have time!" was my reply. Hearing her voice was refreshing to me. I began to recount the things that had happened since we had last talked. It was the *Reader's Digest* condensed version, but I made an effort to hit on the high points of the past year. As I moved closer to the present in my narrative, I told her about the birth of our third son. I can still remember my exact words and her response to them.

"Jonathan was born about six weeks ago," I began, "and I was actually depressed for a few weeks after we came home from the hospital."

There was complete silence at the other end of the line. Then my friend started to laugh. "When you said 'depressed,' I was really worried for just a minute. Then I remembered that depression for you is mild euphoria for the rest of the world."

I had to laugh myself. As I mentioned earlier, I am a woman of high energy and high enthusiasm. That is the way God wired me. I see the glass half full, and actually, I wonder why there is even a question about the quantity of liquid! But there's more to explain my attitude than just my inborn personality.

I am the adult child of an alcoholic. I could tell you story after story of the pain that was caused in my life by a father who drank to excess. He was a professional and respected in the community, and he was an alcoholic. His behavior, his choices affected my life greatly as a child and as an adult. But interestingly enough, I would have to say that it was my mother whose response to our situation had a profound impact on me.

She was a glass-half-empty woman. She was a woman who lived life waiting for, expecting, and perhaps even relishing the possibility of a disaster, natural or otherwise. And when it came to an "otherwise" disaster, my dad did not usually disappoint her.

On occasion I have explained her attitude in life by saying she not only viewed the glass as half empty, but furthermore asked that the glass be removed from the table immediately, before it could leave a mark! Depression for her was *very* real and *very* difficult and I determined early on that when it came to me, it would NOT be *very* contagious. I built upon my naturally optimistic nature. Hence my reported "depression" was more like mild euphoria. And yet I knew as I talked with my old friend that my heart had been hurt.

Years after the phone call that reminded me of the immense difference between my outlook and that of my mother, I came to the realization that through the grace of God, she was my inspiration. I do what I do . . . I write books and speak where invited . . . I encourage women to sing the song God has put inside of them . . . to live life intentionally . . . to make the next right choice regardless of circumstances or choices in the past. I do what I do because my mother did not have that encouragement and she went to her grave with her song unsung.

It was my mother who shaped me, molded me, and inadvertently gave me a purpose bigger than myself. She was also the one who allowed me to live out the words attributed to C. S. Lewis: "Be kind. Everyone you meet is fighting a battle."

And a little reminder to all of you might be in order here. "Everyone" includes the glass-half-empty woman and the glass-half-full woman. Both can have hurting hearts. The battle for that second woman will simply appear more pleasant, more like mild euphoria.

....

KENDRA SMILEY, a former Illinois Mother of the Year, is the mother of three grown sons and has three beloved daughters-in-law. She and her husband, John, live on a working farm in East Central Illinois and enjoy writing and speaking together. She hosts the daily radio program *Live Life Intentionally*, speaks nationally and internationally, and has written nine books, including *Do Your Kids a Favor . . . Love Your Spouse* and *Journey of a Strong-Willed Child*.

WE CAN DO GREAT THINGS
BECAUSE OF WHO *HE* IS

*2 Corinthians 12:9 (NLT): So now I am glad to boast
about my weaknesses, so that the power of Christ
may work through me.*

Little Ol' Me

 I was the runt of the litter. My older sister and brother were strong and athletic. Even my little sister was bigger than I was.

Growing up was a struggle. I struggled physically, academically, socially. I was average at best. No matter how hard I tried, I always ended up somewhere in the middle or below—never at the top.

In spite of my weaknesses, I was blessed. I had godly parents who loved me and taught me about God's love. Our family attended church twice on Sunday every week. Nothing kept my parents from bringing us to church—neither rain, nor sleet, nor snow, and, since we lived in Michigan, there was plenty of that!

I have to confess, I didn't always love going to church. Sometimes it went on too long. Sometimes it was boring. Sometimes I didn't understand one word the preacher was saying. But somewhere along the way, I learned that I was God's child and that He created me. I learned that God loved me enough to die for me—and that He did just that! My Sunday school teacher said that Jesus would have died for me even if I were the only person on earth. That made me feel pretty special.

I survived the growing up years and wanted to be a teacher. Even though I studied hard, I still earned just average grades during my first two years of college. Then in my junior year something happened. Everything began to make sense, and I had a passion for learning like never before. My professors said I was a natural born teacher, and my GPA rose like the morning sun.

After graduating from college, I married my sweetheart and tried to get a teaching job, but there were no jobs to be had. "You have no experience," I was told over and over again.

How was I supposed to get experience if no one would hire me? I finally accepted the only job offer that I had—a teacher's aide position in a nursery school.

Untangling knots from shoelaces, comforting crying children, and wiping noses and toilet seats was not what I had in mind when I pursued a teaching career. I decided I would look for another job. But another job never came along and somewhere between coloring happy faces on orange paper pumpkins and gluing Cheerios onto green paper Christmas trees, I fell in love with my job as well as with the kids.

I'm not sure when or how it happened, but I think it was the day that Katie made me a heart that said "I Wuv You." Or it may have been the time when Jeffrey asked me to marry him. Whenever or however it happened—it was wonderful. The most wonderful thing was that I finally discovered who God created me to be. Whenever I needed a song, poem, or story for a specific theme or lesson, I wrote it myself. Since those were the days before the Internet and information at your fingertips, it was easier for me to make up my own material than spend hours in the library searching for the right thing.

After teaching preschool for five years, I began my years as a stay-at-home mom—loving, teaching, and nurturing my own three little ones. I poured my heart and soul into raising my children, but they didn't stay little for long, and before I knew it they were off to college. I continued to write songs, poems, and stories for little ones and became a published author. It didn't happen overnight, but it *did* happen because that is what God created me to do.

I am humbled and amazed at what God has allowed me to do with my writing, and what He has done through me. I believe that God chooses the weak, so that He is the one who receives the recognition He alone deserves. Without God working in and through me, I am nothing.

Do you ever feel weak? Do you struggle with feelings of inadequacy or wonder who you are? The answer, my friend, is that you are God's child. He loves you enough to die for you. And He can do big things through you, just like He has done through little ol' me!

. . . .

CRYSTAL BOWMAN is a bestselling author of over fifty books for children, including *The One Year Book of Devotions for Preschoolers, The House in the Middle of Town,* and *J Is for Jesus.* She has also written several books for moms as well as magazine articles and lyrics for children's piano music. She speaks at churches, schools, and conferences, and is a mentor at her local MOPS group in Florida. She and her husband have been married for thirty-five years and have three grown children. Her website is www.crystalbowman.com.

DON'T LOSE GOD'S GIFT
OF FRIENDSHIP IN A
WHIRLWIND OF PROJECTS

Philippians 2: 2 (AMP): Fill up and complete my joy
by living in harmony and being of the same mind and one in purpose,
having the same love, being in full accord and of one
harmonious mind and intention.

Saying Good-bye to My Friend Regina

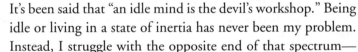

It's been said that "an idle mind is the devil's workshop." Being idle or living in a state of inertia has never been my problem. Instead, I struggle with the opposite end of that spectrum—busyness. Having too much on your plate and the frustration that comes with meeting deadlines, completing projects, and organizing tasks can eat away at the very significance of life. I recently learned that lesson the hard way.

Our heavenly Father is very concerned about our relationships. It's clear from His Word that friendships are precious gifts that should be handled with love and gratitude.

Proverbs 27:17 reminds us that iron sharpens iron. Our true friends and constant companions should be people who share our values and help us cope when times get tough. They share our triumphs and they help us bear up under the weight of sorrow. But they should also be willing to correct us when we're going off course . . . without fear of losing the friendship.

Regina was that kind of friend. We grew up together and played silly children's games under the streetlights until our parents called us home. We both had older and younger siblings, who all attended the same elementary and junior high schools. Church was so close to our homes that the neighborhood kids walked to services. I remember Regina in Sunday school. She had a megawatt smile and the kind of warmth that made her easy to love. Though we lost touch as both our families moved to different neighborhoods, I never forgot her.

The years went by as rapidly as rushing waters traversing a winding creek. In high school, I met my friend again. We attempted to pick up where we'd left off, but time got away from us and before we knew it, we were graduating and moving on to college. I didn't see Regina for many years after that.

I entered college, focused on my studies, doing all I could to meet my goals. By God's grace, I got my degree, and a dream job that came with a ton of responsibilities. Regina also got her degree and became very successful. We lived in neighboring states. I moved from the city to the suburbs and one day, as I walked into church, there was Regina! She'd married one of our high school classmates, and some years after the birth of their daughter, God spoke to their hearts about adopting eight children.

Regina and I rekindled our friendship and spent many hours catching up. She'd suggest weekend get-togethers, but I was always too busy. She was a much better manager of her time, even with such great responsibilities. She'd quit her job to dedicate herself to her children, but she was still willing to make time for me. We'd have an occasional lunch, but we both hungered for more fellowship. My projects kept getting in the way, and because I talk for a living, the phone was not my favorite form of communication. Eventually, I left the church we attended, got married, moved back to the city, and began a new phase in my life. But when Regina and her husband didn't show up for my wedding, I knew something was wrong.

That's when I learned my friend was sick, really sick. She didn't send word about her illness until she was about to be moved from a hospital to hospice. We spoke on the phone, her voice weakened by the cancer that had overtaken her body. I shared my heart and she shared hers. On the day I had plans to go see her, to embrace her and to tell her I loved her . . . she died.

I don't doubt she's with our Lord, but I miss my friend. And I'm angry with myself for not doing a better job of keeping in touch. A simple phone call might have given her comfort. A visit might have eased her pain. Her family asked me to speak at her funeral. I was happy to do so . . . and as I did, I made a promise to God that I'd never again allow my busyness to rob me of the gift of friendship.

Eric Hoffer once put it this way: "The feeling of being hurried is not usually the result of living a full life and having no time. It is, on the contrary, born of a vague fear that we are wasting our life. When we do not do the one thing we ought to do, we have no time for anything else—we are the busiest people in the world." That'll never happen to me again.

FELICIA MIDDLEBROOKS HILL is one of the top media personalities in Chicago, anchoring the award-winning morning drive program on CBS Radio 780 for a record twenty-five years. She is also a filmmaker; her documentary, *Somebody's Child: The Redemption of Rwanda*, took top honors at a New York film festival in 2005. She coauthored *Called*, about United Flight 93, which crashed over Pennsylvania on September 11, 2001. She founded Saltshaker Productions, LLC, with offices in Los Angeles and Chicago. She's on the boards of several nonprofits and teaches journalism at Purdue University and DePaul University.

NEVER UNDERESTIMATE GOD'S POWER
TO SURPRISE YOU WITH HIS
GOODNESS AND LOVE

Hebrews 12:1 (NIV): Therefore, since we are surrounded
by such a great cloud of witnesses, let us throw off everything
that hinders and the sin that so easily entangles, and let us
run with perseverance the race marked out for us.

Running to the Finish Line

 I stood in the Florida morning sun, camera poised for the best shot of Steve and our oldest daughter, Lauren. Seconds later the runners leading the pack began pounding past me to the finish line just yards to my left. I strained to see if Steve and Lauren were behind them, but couldn't see them yet.

Of course, they wouldn't be first. I knew that. Just running at all, much less together in this race, was huge. I wanted a newspaper reporter to show up, even a high school band. I settled for telling someone who looked like the race organizer. "You know my husband and our daughter are running together today. It's the first time he's run since his heart attack two years ago."

"Oh yeah?" He barely looked at me. "That's nice."

I wasn't done yet. "Yes, and my daughter flew down from Buffalo, New York, just to run in this race. And she has lupus." That got his attention.

"No kidding. That's amazing."

I could have told him more, but runners were heading my way in small herds now. I had to have the camera ready. I waited, remembering how impossible I would have thought this day just two years ago when Steve emerged from his bypass surgery looking nearly gone for good, like Aslan on the Stone Table. While complications threatened his recovery, our whole family and countless friends prayed fervently for God's healing mercy. Gradually it came, and my once strong husband, the image of athleticism, began crawling toward recovery. And now, today . . .

Here they were! Rounding the bend, pumping hard, faces heated, but talking to each other as they raced to the finish line. What were they saying? I wanted to cheer and jump for joy, but tried to stand still and hold the camera steady as they kicked past me.

I never noticed the rest of the runners coming in. Tears clouded my view as I watched Lauren and Steve walking arm in arm past the finish line and around the parking lot together, cooling down, heads bowed slightly, praying.

Not long ago, no one would have believed this possible for Lauren either, who was often bedridden with lupus, on prednisone daily, trying to care for two small children. Her husband, Michael, worked from a home office to help with the family. Then Lauren got pregnant with a third child, a huge surprise. Was she strong enough to carry this baby, even to care for it? I worried. We all did.

But God did a miracle, in fact many miracles that year. Not only was little Kerith Brooke born perfectly healthy after many obstacles, but Lauren entered a remission from lupus that continues to this day. I watched her now, looking strong and healthy again, thrilled at the sight. Could it last? We pray so, but for today I joined a crowd of heaven's onlookers cheering them both on, leaping for joy at the serendipitous gifts God gives when we least expect them.

"Hi, Mom!" Lauren finally saw me and waved. With her long blonde ponytail tucked inside a ball cap, she looked like the ten-year-old I remembered.

"Stay there, you two," I said. "I want this picture. It's a great one." Snapping their two wide grins, I asked, "Hey, what were you two talking about as you came around the bend?"

"Dad was telling me to pump a little harder toward the finish line. I didn't think I could do it, but I did."

"I knew she could," Steve said proudly. And she did. Minutes later, when the times were posted, Lauren won a bronze medal in her age category. Her first ever. My vision fogged up again.

I need that picture in my mind today. A new health challenge faces our family and threatens my peace each day as my dear sister-in-law lies gravely ill with a possible recurrence of cancer. It tears me apart, but I pray daily and surrender the outcome to God who loves us more than we can begin to fathom. I'm learning He has surprises waiting at every bend in the road as we run to our finish line. He probably has cheerleaders and a band ready, too.

VIRELLE KIDDER is a seasoned communicator who loves speaking and writing about the reality of knowing God. She is the author of six books, including *The Best Life Ain't Easy* and *Meet Me at the Well*, and countless articles published worldwide. Virelle and her husband, Steve, have four grown children and eight grandchildren, and live in Sebastian, Florida. Visit Virelle at www.virellekidder.com and sign up for her newsletter, "Virelle & Friends."

GOD WILL MAKE MY
SECRET PAIN INTO
SOMETHING BEAUTIFUL

Psalm 38:9 (NIV): All my longings lie open
before you, O Lord; my sighing is not hidden from you.

A Secret Club

My husband had gone to a meeting at church and my children were asleep down the hall when a stranger entered my bedroom, waking me from a deep sleep. Through the dim light reflecting from the hallway, I saw his silhouette—and vaguely understood that a tall man with thick arms stood a few feet away.

I didn't scream. For a few seconds, I didn't really understand what was happening. "Who are you?" I asked.

I might have rolled over and disappeared back into my dreams, but the ugliness of his laugh shocked me into wakefulness. I sat up quickly, and he yanked a knife out of his pocket.

"Oh no," I whispered, holding my hands up toward him as if sheer willpower would keep him away. "No. Don't do this."

Someone once told me that after she was raped she felt like she joined a secret club she never wanted to be part of. I cried when she said it, because it was true for me too. Suddenly I knew things in a profound way I didn't want to know at all—things like shame and doubt and fear. And I knew how much ugliness there was in this world.

The overpowering emotions I experienced didn't go away the next month, or even the next year—but neither did my community. Like every good church, mine had an impromptu "casserole committee"—when a member was hurting, the others rushed in with food. I hadn't much understood this casserole obsession until I was its beneficiary and discovered that hot meals made by loving hands comfort the soul better than Band-Aids on skinned knees. All the little acts of service—from lawn mowing to housecleaning to babysitting—said what I needed to hear: "I love you." "You are one of us." "We're in this with you." Slowly I began to notice more joy than despair, more confidence than fear. And so much love was poured into me that there was no room left for shame.

One of the tokens of kindness given to me at that time was a puppy. This darling little beagle proved remarkably protective and became our family's watchdog. I went outside one bright winter day to find little Gus growling menacingly. I looked around to see what was threatening him, but didn't notice a thing out of place. Feeling a little spooked, I stroked his ears, hoping to calm him; but he bared his teeth and raised his hackles. Then I saw it, the menacing figure that Gus kept at bay: A great—big—snowman.

It took awhile to convince my small protector that this intruder was no threat. I pulled off the orange hat from the snowman's head and tossed its raisin eyes and carrot nose in Gus's direction. He ate them, and moved slowly forward. By the time I had yanked the sticks out of the snowman's sides and the scarf from its neck, Gus saw the wilting lump of snow for what it really was: an empty threat.

My community disassembled my "snowman." They helped me to see that my hackle-raising fear of physical harm, and the even greater suspicion that my faith had been wrongly placed, was unnecessary. I had not been abandoned by God, and His people proved it.

It has been over a decade since the rape, and I've experienced many life changes since then. I gave birth to a precious baby girl, conceived that fateful night, and she is now my daily reminder of God's restorative love. We adopted a little boy we knew from the inner-city neighborhood where we lived—and he now towers over me, a godly young man who brings much laughter to our family. Eight years after the rape, my husband, who had joined me in joyously welcoming our daughter and who still loves her today, suddenly abandoned the marriage—and I am now building a new home and blended family. I've moved from Michigan to Colorado to Indiana. I've experienced the death of loved ones and the birth of a grandchild. Yet through all those changes, one thing has remained constant in my life: God's faithful love. And I see now how much more beauty exists in this world than ugliness, even when life is hard.

I don't know what secret club you have joined, but I am confident that God is in it with you, loving you and drawing you to Him. I pray that you too will be startled by beauty.

HEATHER GEMMEN WILSON is the author of *Startling Beauty: My Journey from Rape to Restoration* and speaks internationally on the subject of hope and forgiveness. Visit her website at www.heathergemmen.com.

GOD KEEPS ME GOING

*Isaiah 43:1–3 (THE MESSAGE): Don't be afraid,
I've redeemed you. I've called your name.
You're mine. When you're in over your head,
I'll be there with you. When you're in rough waters,
you will not go down. When you're between a rock
and a hard place, it won't be a dead end—
because I am God, your personal God."*

Between a Rock and a Hard Place

I call my husband my two-year wonder, because every two years I wonder what he is going to do next. In not quite twenty-four years of marriage, Rich's life changes—including twelve companies, four careers, three surgeries, and three relocations—have significantly affected my life. Along the way, I have personally experienced God's amazing provision of grace, flexibility, and all good things.

Internally wired to be spontaneous and enjoy variety, I am a good fit for this marriage. I like change. However, when Rich announced one Sunday morning sixteen years ago that he was finished with God—well, that change rattled me to the core. You see, I married him straight out of Bible college when he passionately loved God. He worked with kids as a youth pastor in one church for two years and a second church for an additional two years before going into business. This newest change was not in my plan book and I could not imagine how it could be in God's plans either.

Fast-forward a few years to a Wednesday afternoon when, out of the blue, our seven-year-old daughter suddenly said to me, "Half my heart believes in Jesus, but the other half doesn't know if He's real. What do I do, Mom?" My own heart seemed to leap into my throat. Then I became angry.

I lashed out first, mentally, at my husband. *How could you do this to our child? It's your fault she can't see God. Why can't you be the godly father she needs? You caused this!*

But then my mind turned to God. *You knew this would happen. You see and know all. Why did You allow us to have a child in this situation? You could have stopped this. You could have . . .* And then I realized who I was talking to. Remorse and sorrow filled me. I spoke to Him again with a contrite heart. *Forgive me, Lord. Please show me how to guide Becky. I need You.*

God led us to verses that confirmed Becky's faith. Over the next few days and weeks, Becky's daily prayer requests reflected her earnest search for God. And He showed up. He answered Becky's prayer requests in marvelous God-ways. We both saw Him at work in her life and in the world around us.

Today I treasure this story because I know God intentionally used Rich's lack of faith to help Becky question and build her own. She might not own today the solid conviction that God is God if she had not proved Him faithful almost ten years ago. I humbly thank God for her journey and strong faith. And we still pray together that Rich's faith might one day rival our own!

The journey is still so difficult. Sixteen years and counting is a long time to wait for an answer to prayer. A long time to hover between a rock and a hard place. But this is not a dead end. Although it has been a long time to tread water in a rough ocean, I'm not going down. Because God is personal. He walks with me *through* the difficulties of life—for my good and His glory.

I will praise Him today, tomorrow, and forever for His personal love and redemption. I know that I would not go back and change anything, because the growth in my life and in Becky's is so very valuable. I grieve for and pray unceasingly for Rich. And with his permission, I share our story and my faith, watching with profound joy as others find hope to hold on in despair and disappointment to the One who is personally involved and provides every need.

. . . .

NANCY SEBASTIAN MEYER vulnerably writes and speaks about the ups and downs of marriage to a pastor-turned-agnostic—who allows her to share their story. She is the author of several books, including *Spiritually Single Moms: Raising Godly Kids When Dad Doesn't Believe* and *Beyond Expectations: Finding Joy in Your Marriage.* Nancy shares God's truth with women who need hope. She and her family live in Lancaster, Pennsylvania. www.nancysebastianmeyer.com

Do you feel like you're in over your head? Be assured that as a child of God, you have a protective Redeemer, patient Savior, and most personal God. Look at Him. Grab His hand and allow Him to hold on to you. Feel the security of His grip, the warmth of His love, and the tenderness of His care. Someday you will look back to see the purpose of His refining work in your life. For now, grab hold of the Savior, find your footing, and then look around and behold the blessings of this moment.

GOD'S PRESENCE IS ALWAYS NEAR

John 3:16 (NIV): For God so loved the
world that he gave his one and only Son,
that whoever believes in him
shall not perish but have eternal life.

Rainbows — The Language of God

The unexpected moments in life sometimes seem so over-whelming that we can lose the sense of God's presence and His purpose for our lives. During those times of turmoil, I have discovered an effective coping method: Prayer, or as I call it, "my conversations with God." Although I enjoy the formal prayers within church, I feel closest to God when I just talk to Him. Communication is essential to a strong relationship, and He provides an unlimited calling plan to each of us.

As chairperson of WINGS (Women in Need Growing Stronger), a nonprofit organization that helps homeless women and children, predominantly victims of domestic violence, I saw a real need in our community to build a safe house. I felt that this was one of God's purposes in my life—providing a place of shelter and safety to women who flee a dangerous situation at home, even during the middle of the night. Yet the red tape of bureaucracy and legal proceedings continued to post a potential dead end to these efforts. The possibility of losing the safe house was upsetting. While driving to yet another hearing on this matter, I experienced one of those overwhelming moments and called out to God. "Why isn't this happening? It's a real need in the suburbs to help these women and frightened children have a safe place to go. What else do I need to do?"

I will never forget His answer. I looked into the sky and saw a gorgeous rainbow stretched across the grayness of the afternoon. The rainbow's end appeared to shine over the building where the meeting would take place. That day, WINGS received the official go-ahead to build the safe house, and I learned an important lesson. God promises that He is always with us. His perfect plan in His perfect timing stretches across the grayness of our lives with a "rainbow reminder" that He is there. He is God. All things are possible through Him. Today, WINGS has a safe house in the Chicago suburbs that in 2005/2006 served 83 women and 81 children who received 5,610 nights of shelter and supportive services.

RITA CANNING graduated from the University of Illinois, Champaign, with a bachelor of science from the College of Commerce and Business Administration. She is Chairperson of WINGS and founder of the Palatine Home of the Sparrow, which are transitional shelter programs for abused and homeless women and their children. She is also a member of the women's board of Northwestern University, the women's board of the Field Museum, a director of Harris Bank—Palatine, a director of the Buehler YMCA, and a trustee at Harper College. Rita and her husband, John, live in the Chicago area and have six children. She enjoys tennis, golf, and racquetball.

Yes, I realize that in every dark circumstance I will not encounter a physical rainbow. However, I can appreciate the significance of that colorful prism and remember its message. "Whenever the rainbow appears in the clouds, I will see it and remember the everlasting covenant between God and all living creatures of every kind on the earth" (Genesis 9:16). God spoke these words to Noah after he and his family left the ark, their safe house during the terrible flood.

I don't think God meant that there would no longer be emotional and physical floods. However, I do believe that the rainbow reminds us of God's covenant and commitment and that He is our Safe House during our darkest moments. His right arm is the rainbow stretched across the grayness of our lives as He holds us from heaven.

GOD CARES ABOUT YOUR BODY

Matthew 6:26 (NIV): Look at the birds of the air;
they do not sow or reap or store away in barns,
and yet your heavenly Father feeds them.
Are you not much more valuable than they?

My Weight Loss—A Heart Change

I had outpatient surgery in January 2008. When I eased myself out of the recovery bed, the nurse who was helping me commented, "You're so tiny."

"Thanks," I replied, pausing and wondering if I should tell her my news. "I recently lost fifty pounds," I confessed.

"You should write a book about that," she suggested.

"Funny you say that. I'm an author," I replied, telling her about my new book at the time, *Stories of Faith and Courage from the Revolutionary War.*

Modern-day fitness and the Revolutionary War don't have much in common. However, John Adams made an interesting observation about the meaning of a revolution. He concluded that America's Revolution was more than just a war. It was a changing of hearts and minds. If his definition is true, then my weight loss in 2007 was a genuine revolution.

After getting married in 1994, I steadily gained weight. I lost some here and there, but I could never deprive myself of all the food I loved long enough to lose the weight. Something deep inside of me changed after giving birth to my second son in 2007. My pregnancy was difficult.

I was on bed rest for eighty-nine days. I came out of that reclusive time determined to live life differently. When I got on the scales a few weeks after Zachary's birth, I was astonished at the ugly number staring at me. When I looked up my healthy weight range based on age, height, and bone structure, I bawled. I had only gained twenty-five pounds with pregnancy, but I had started that pregnancy twenty-five pounds higher than my healthy weight range. I cried for days.

What made the difference this time around was my desperation. I prayed to God for direction. I was willing to do whatever He asked me to do. He gently reminded me that He truly cares about my body and wants me to care about it as well. Doctors have come up with healthy weight ranges based on reasonable standards. It made sense to me that God created a healthy weight boundary for my four-foot, eleven-inch body size. Fifty pounds is a lot of extra weight for my height. I knew His love for me was not dependent on my appearance, but I also knew His love for me was a great reason to get the weight off.

I also discovered that God has given us an often-overlooked, built-in weight manager: hunger. Hunger became my best friend and compass. I learned to wait to eat until I was hungry and stopped when I was full. This resulted in a sharp cut in my portions. I also stopped turning to food to satisfy my emotions or boredom. Prayer proved more effective in those moments. Weighing myself daily and drinking water kept me accountable. I soon began desiring fresh and healthy foods, lean meats, fruits, and vegetables. I allowed myself to eat chocolate, but saved it for when I was hungry. I also took up Pilates and Body & Soul, a nationwide aerobic exercise and strength-training class.

I had tried standardized programs before, with some success, but I usually couldn't make the changes I needed to in my heart and mind. I couldn't wait to get off the diet and back to eating the way I wanted. That kind of thinking is not a weight-loss revolution. One reason I know I have truly changed is this: I have no desire to return to my previous habits.

Just as God has made each of us unique, so He's also given us a unique way to manage and care for our bodies. The nuances of what works for me may not work best for someone else.

However, I believe weight management is a heart, mind, and soul issue. To change our bodies on the outside requires a change of heart and mind on the inside. That's the way God designed us. He uses heart changes to make a difference—even revolutionize—other areas of our lives. When I overturned the prison of my eating habits to God, I walked out in freedom. God radically altered this area of my life because He changed my heart. My weight loss was an inside-out process.

Bestselling author and columnist **JANE HAMPTON COOK** is known for making history both memorable and relevant to today's news, political events, and issues of faith. A former webmaster for President George W. Bush, she served two years as White House deputy director of Internet news services and three years in the Texas governor's office. Her books, columns, and speeches deliver prolific portrayals of modern-day heroes and historic Americans, particularly the Founding Fathers, U.S. presidents, and the nation's first ladies. She is the author of *Stories of Faith and Courage from the Revolutionary War* and *The Faith of America's First Ladies.* (www.janecook.com)

STEP OUT ON FAITH

Romans 8:28 (KJV): And we know that all things
work together for good to them that love God,
to them who are the called according to his purpose.

Let God and Let Go

 The hospital was eerily familiar. Looking down the hallways at the kids in wheelchairs reminded me of the races we had up and down the corridors. Peering into the small, colorful, hospital classroom, I almost expected to see my tutor telling me to double-check my arithmetic.

When I turned a corner and suddenly saw the giant doors of the operating room, I shuddered involuntarily. This was the room where they amputated my right leg. I can still clearly remember being wheeled down that long corridor through that swinging entryway. I remember how cold the table was when my skin touched the metal through the open back of the hospital gown.

I thought I would never be able to close my eyes and then, after it seemed only an instant had passed, I found myself in the recovery room with a mass of bandages where my deformed foot used to be. Phantom pains made me want to wiggle or scratch toes that no longer existed. Other more intense pains would often overwhelm me at night so that a nurse would have to wake me up to stop me from screaming. I was only five years old.

I shook off these heavy thoughts and returned to the present. I was no longer that frightened child. The Shriners Hospital had provided free of charge all the surgeries, artificial legs, and therapy that I needed. But it was more than my body that needed healing.

God worked through the hands of the many nurses who brushed my hair, wiped away my tears, and sat with me during painful hours of rehabilitation. They not only taught me to walk, but to walk tall and feel good about myself. When Jesus did miracles, He told the people: "If the Father can do this for your body, just think what He can do for your soul!" Indeed, God's strength repaired my leg, but moreover His love repaired my heart.

I left with not only the ability to walk and run and play on my new leg, but with the confidence to learn to ski. Eventually I qualified for the U.S. Paralympic ski team and won a silver and two bronze medals. I was the second fastest one-legged skier in the world—and the first African-American ever to win an Olympic medal in ski racing!

So I came back to the hospital wearing my Olympic jacket, my medals, and shorts that proudly showed off my high tech sports leg with the hydraulic knee joint. I came to thank the Shriners, thank the nurses, and even more important, to serve as an inspiration to the current crop of frightened boys and girls. I wanted to help let them know that their future could be filled with promise, opportunity, and joy.

In the corridor outside the patient rooms, I saw a young girl using a walker; one of her feet was artificial. Since neither she nor her mother spoke very much English, I explained in my broken Spanish that I had been a patient in the hospital when I was about her age. The girl looked at me and then slowly lifted her pants leg to show me that her real foot was still there—sticking out in the middle of her shin above the artificial foot. I realized that her disability was probably similar to mine. My foot had been amputated so that it wouldn't stick out like that.

A translator came over to help us talk. "Are you thinking about getting a leg like mine?" I asked.

"Oh no!" her mother said. "She wants to keep her foot."

There was so much I wanted to tell her about how great life would be without using a walker and about all the wonderful new technology available in prosthetics. My journey had been long and hard, but so worthwhile. I looked into the eyes of that little girl and saw the same fears I had when I was her age. How could I tell them? How to explain the power of God's love to heal body and spirit?

I showed her. I ran down the hallway as fast as I could. When I reached the end, I turned around and ran back. I took out the jump rope I had in my bag and jumped rope. When words failed, I used my body itself to communicate.

I couldn't see her face the whole time, but someone told me later that her eyes were as big as saucers. I hope that God used me to help her trust Him. I felt as though He sent me there that day to deliver a message to that little girl.

It is so easy for me to see God's love at work in her life. By some miracle she has been brought from Mexico to this state-of-the-art hospital where everything she needs is completely free. Yet, she is reluctant to accept help because she wants to hold on to a foot that doesn't work.

I see myself in that little girl. Not because we have the same physical disability, but because I know that even after all the miracles I have experienced, I still find it hard to have the courage to completely trust God in my life. So many times God must have looked at me like a child who doesn't understand when I cling to what I have instead of trusting Him to give me so much more.

Is there a "foot" you are holding on to in your life that is blocking your blessings? God has everything prepared for us but so often we can be like a small child from a foreign country who can't see the big picture.

I pray that little girl will let go and let God. At the same time, I pray that I can continue to deepen my own faith and stop clinging to the things that block my own blessings.

BONNIE ST. JOHN. Having her right leg amputated at age five began a series of challenges that might have destroyed Bonnie had she not learned to pray. A professional speaker who has appeared on the *Today Show, CNN,* the *700 Club,* and *Life Today* as well as being featured in *People,* the *New York Times,* and *Essence,* she is committed to reaching out to the world with a message of triumph over circumstance. Bonnie is the author of *How Strong Women Pray* and *Live Your Joy.* For more information you can visit www.bonniestjohn.com or read her blog at www.bonniestjohn.com/blog.aspx.

THERE IS HEALING IN BROKENNESS

2 Corinthians 12:9 (NLT): "My grace is all you need. My power works best
in weakness." So now I am glad to boast about my weaknesses,
so that the power of Christ can work through me.

Finding God in the Waves
of Change and Brokenness

 While growing up I was a girl with big dreams. I was going to marry
Prince Charming, raise perfect kids, and be successful. After all, I
had a God who loved me, and a loving and supportive family.

By God's grace I did meet my Prince Charming. In the span of a year
and half, we married, had a premature baby, and graduated from college.
Jobs were scarce at this time, and the most significant life-changing event was
moving across the United States away from my family, friends, and church.

How was I going to become somebody when I was a new wife and
mother in a strange land? I didn't know anybody and no one knew me.

We began our new life anxiously waiting to see where God would
lead. My husband was blessed with a steady job but we began living a life
we could not afford. Credit card debt and bills piled up faster than we
could pay. My husband accepted a higher paying job. Surely having more
money would solve our problems. But within one year he was let go.

Previously, when the storms of life turned me upside down, I turned
to family and friends, but God had moved me away from everyone I
relied on. I've heard it said that "When man plans, God laughs." I felt
God was laughing at the girl with big dreams. My kids were not perfect,
I was not *somebody*, and I did not have the white picket fence.

Where had God gone?

Tadd and I were led to a Christian financial advisor for help. I stepped into that office expecting "financial" advice. Instead, this godly man through God's Word broke every barrier I had built around my heart: the wall of low self-image, the wall of insecurity, and the wall of feeling unworthy of God's grace and love. I was taught God is a jealous God and wanted me to abide in Him only, not in my circumstances. I left the office that day shattered and sobbing. I cried myself into an exhausted sleep that night.

I was angry about things not going my way. How dare God move me away from everything and everyone familiar! But He knew I was trying to look good on the outside, while I was dying on the inside. Playing "Christian" wore me out. I still loved Jesus and believed He was there, *somewhere.*

My husband's strength and encouragement kept me from blowing away. We began the slow and difficult journey of paying off our debt and living within our means. When I turned to God's Word, He said, "My grace is all you need. My power works best in weakness." I felt weak from life's storms, and needed a lot of God's grace.

In the midst of renewing my walk with Christ, God led us to a new church and I began a study of the apostle Paul's life. He was a man who was beaten, rejected, shipwrecked, and left for dead, but God used him to spread the gospel. If God used a broken man like Paul, I felt there was still hope for this broken girl.

If you find yourself shattered by the waves of life, our Yahweh-Raphah, the "Lord who heals," is calling you to come. My life was capsized and did not go according to my plan, but God's grace carried me through the waves of change and brokenness. God was not laughing at my big dreams, He was teaching me to abide in Him. He used these storms to develop a greater reliance in Him.

Are you broken? Burned out? God takes your pain and suffering and develops it into a thing of beauty. God is calling you to walk with Him and soak in the waters of grace and mercy.

LORI KASBEER is the book reviewer for *Christian Women Online* magazine. She has a house full of boys; three to be exact, however, if you add her husband, the cat, and the dog, testosterone runs rapid. With a heart for women, she finds it a privilege to remind women today that God is deeply in love with them.

JESUS IS OUR GUIDE

John 14:6 (THE MESSAGE): Jesus said,
"I am the Road, also the Truth, also the Life.
No one gets to the Father apart from me."

Getting Lost and Found

My name is Jennifer and I am directionally challenged.

While I am good at a lot of things, navigating isn't one of them. Hand me a map, or even turn-by-turn directions and send me on my way but give me your cell phone number. No matter how good the directions are, I am likely to get lost—not so lost that I can't be found, but just lost enough to make me anxious.

I guess that's because I drive by feel. If the GPS says I am headed east, but I *feel* like we're headed north, then I assume the GPS is acting up. If I *feel* like I should turn right, I turn right, even if the directions tell me to continue on the road I'm on.

Sometimes my spiritual life can also be directionally challenged. I think I know where I am going, I can even *feel* it, but somehow I take a wrong turn and I head in the wrong direction.

One day Jordan, my four-year-old, said. "I can't wait until Sunday."

Sunday was Easter, so I knew what he was thinking about. "Are you excited about coloring eggs and getting candy in your basket?"

"No, I can't wait until Sunday because that's when Jesus rises from the dead."

While I am dreaming of chocolate rabbits and colored eggs, Jordan is focused on Jesus. How did I get so off track?

Determined to make it right, I took that opportunity to explain to Jordan that Jesus wasn't rising from the dead *this* Sunday. I told him how Jesus lived two thousand years ago, how He died, and how three days after His death He was raised from the dead. "Ever since then," I explained, "Jesus has been in heaven with God."

"Ooh," he said in that voice that meant he understood. I was proud of myself; perhaps I was back on the right road after all. But then Jordan added, "I still don't get it."

I wasn't sure I could make it any clearer to him, but then I had an idea. "We have to go to the bookstore. While we're there, we'll get a book with pictures that will tell the whole story. We can read it together, okay?"

I had seen some Easter picture books just a few days earlier and I was proud of myself for thinking of a solution so quickly. But Jordan had an even better idea. "Can't we just read it out of the Bible?"

I wish this off-road religious experience were the only time this happened, but it wasn't.

One day my friend Kari called and said she was considering a divorce. Her husband had been unfaithful and unrepentant. She wanted to know what I thought she should do. I told her I wanted to be sure of God's will for her in this situation, promised her I would do a little research, pray about it, and call her back in a couple of days. I hung up and immediately got to work.

Now for most Christians, this would mean pulling out a Bible and maybe a concordance or commentary. But that isn't what I did. I went to the computer to see what Christian websites had to say about divorce.

Why? Because it just felt like the right thing to do.

I'm used to Googling for information when I need it, so this time without thinking I took a wrong turn and went to the Internet for spiritual guidance. I am embarrassed to admit that it took almost ninety minutes and looking at a lot of contradictory advice, before it finally occurred to me that I should have gone directly to the Bible to see what

God had to say about divorce, not what *others* had to say about what the Bible said.

Have you ever lost your way spiritually? Even temporarily? Perhaps like me, you want to be the knowledgeable one, the expert who can give directions to others when they don't know where to go. But one day you realize that instead of being the guide, it's you who's lost.

When we take spiritual detours, Jesus reminds us that He is the way. And His way is grace. I don't have to be anxious even when I take a wrong turn, because He is there to help me back on the road.

And no one is better at finding those who are lost than He is.

JENNIFER SCHUCHMANN is the coauthor of *Nine Ways God Always Speaks, Six Prayers God Always Answers,* and *Your Unforgettable Life.* She has contributed to *The Church Leader's Answer Book* and the *Couples' Devotional Bible.* She holds an MBA from Emory University and a bachelor's degree in psychology from the University of Memphis. Jennifer and her husband, David, have one son and live in Atlanta where she is almost always lost in a good book. www.jenniferschuchmann.com

IF ONE WOMAN IS DOWN, HER FRIEND CAN HELP HER UP

Colossians 2:2 (THE MESSAGE): I want you woven into a tapestry of love, in touch with everything there is to know of God. Then you will have minds confident and at rest, focused on Christ, God's great mystery.

"What Goes Around Comes Around"

The proverb implies that what we do or say will eventually come full circle. I've always interpreted the expression as the gloomy warning of a threatening cloud looming overhead, just waiting to burst forth a storm when we least suspect it. But I've discovered that if we do something worth doing, it comes back around as an unexpected blessing, a refreshing shower on a sultry day.

I've also learned that we have to be willing to "take your own medicine" in order to reap the blessing.

I was in my midthirties when I finally stepped foot on a college campus to begin my degree. My daughter was in high school. Widowed, I had recently remarried. We moved from a ranch house in the country to a century-old Victorian home in town. It was a major transition: new future, new husband, new home, new church.

The Victorian home was my husband's: my dream home, his bachelor pad! I couldn't wait to cover those ten-foot walls with paint and paper! When summer break came, I put away the books and the renovations began. I thought I could do it myself, but it was so much work! Old homes present unique problems. In the midsummer heat it was like working in a brick oven. My creative energy was evaporating.

With my husband working long hours, I began to feel overwhelmed.

It wasn't just the project. It was the sense of being alone: a middle-aged newlywed, in a new environment, on a new schedule, in a new town. My daughter now had her driver's license, her own car, her independence. She didn't need me to drive her to ball practice or to a friend's house. There was no one to talk to throughout the day; no one to share my burdens or understand what I was going through.

One day a new friend dropped by. She was a teacher, also on summer break. We were staring at the carpet in the front room. It was stifling, like a giant itchy wool sweater ready to swallow me up. She understood. Better yet, she had a plan and the experience to pull it off. Four hours later, my hubbie came home to beautiful antique oak floors.

The rest of the summer we were a team. I helped redecorate her kitchen, she helped me wallpaper my walls. Though we each had our own "to-do" lists, we accomplished more together than we could ever have done alone.

Soon it was September and back to the books. But the lesson I learned during the summer was invaluable. It exposed my need to connect with women, my longing for deeper relationships. Though I had made new friends at church, every Sunday was the same. We never got beyond "Hi! How are you?" Week after week, I went to church with people I knew only on the surface. I wanted to go beyond hairdos and clothing styles. I wanted to know the hearts of other women.

I discovered that my need was universal, and that God wanted to meet this female need. The answer to my prayer came as a ministry plan with Colossians 2:2 as the mission: "I want you woven into a tapestry of love, in touch with everything there is to know of God."

I envisioned women gathering in homes, becoming intimately acquainted with one another and with the Lord. By being in our personal surroundings, we would become familiar with spouses, children, pets, and actually have something to talk about next time we passed in the halls of church. Most important, we would be an encouragement to one another, become "woven together" as three-dimensional beings rather than competitive opposition. I began to dream about the powerful force we could be as a team.

In January, I hosted our first monthly WoVeN: Women of Virtue Network gathering. Little did I know: the nine of us were training to be group leaders. By October, we spawned four groups with forty-four women. The joy of connecting was contagious! One woman said she never really knew her sister-in-law of twenty-five years until they were in a WoVeN group together. A 24-year-old and 90-year-old became the dearest of friends. We found a safe harbor, a place to share our fears, successes and heartaches; a powerhouse of prayer support.

My call to full-time ministry led me away from that church and into churches across the country and into South Africa. WoVeN went with me, and God has used this ministry to connect women, weaving them into His beautiful tapestry of love.

Ten years later, my story comes full circle. I had poured myself into ministry to the point of burnout and resignation. Waiting for my next assignment, my first priority was rest and recuperation. Now I was the one needing to be ministered to. I was the one in the desert. The temptation was to avoid people, to isolate myself from others until the storm lifted. But the innate longing that originally spurred the WoVeN groups began gnawing at my heart. I had been so immersed in my work; I neglected the friendships that were meaningful to me. I wrote a note to a friend from the initial group that met in my home. To my surprise, she invited me to WoVeN, which was meeting the following week. After all those years, they were still going strong!

CYNTHIA K. STIVERSON'S call to ministry has opened doors to speak at conferences, retreats, and in churches across the U.S. and in South Africa. As founder of Women of Virtue Network, she authored two workbooks, *A Monthly Oasis for Women* and *Entertaining Angels*. Cynthia considers raising her daughter, author-speaker Nicole Bromley, as her greatest accomplishment in life. She resides in Howard, Ohio, with her husband, Mark.

It was a bitter pill to swallow my pride and walk into this group of women, ten years removed, used to ministering to others and now in need of being ministered to. But I'm so glad I took that pill! It was wonderful medicine for my broken spirit, an oasis in my desert. Several of the women had been there from the very beginning. It was a reunion of kindred spirits, hearts "woven into a tapestry of love."

What goes around comes around, but we have to be willing to "take our own medicine"!

FACE LIFE WITH JOY, FAITH,
AND PERSEVERANCE—
NO MATTER WHAT MAY COME

James 1:2–4 (NIV): Consider it pure joy, my brothers,
whenever you face trials of many kinds, because you know
that the testing of your faith develops perseverance.
Perseverance must finish its work so that you may be mature
and complete, not lacking anything.

As Seen on TV!

 I'm thinking of having a badge made with that slogan on it so when people stop me in a store or restaurant and say, "Hey! Didn't I see you on _____?" they can look at the badge and laugh with me. I think it would be a great icebreaker—especially since everyone wants to ask me questions about the shows, or more specifically, "How I do it." Have joy, that is.

But joy hasn't always been easy for me. The Lord definitely had His work cut out for Him when it came to teaching me that lesson.

More than a decade ago, my husband and I were serving at a great church in the south. We loved the church, the teens we worked with, and the close-knit community. But one day my husband, Jeremy, came home and told me that he needed to resign. I briefly thought about asking him if he'd lost his mind, but common sense took over and I knew there had to be a reason.

"I feel like the Lord is telling me to." Yep. That's what he said.

All righty then. I nodded and attempted to put on my supportive-pastor's-wife hat. But inside my heart was a different story. I complained. I whined. I grumbled.

Lord? Are You sure about this? Did You really tell him that?

My husband drove back up to the church to write his resignation. I stomped around the house unloading the dishwasher a little louder than normal, slamming the laundry basket down with much more force than necessary. All the while—ranting at God, "But we have two babies in diapers, we don't have any money, Jeremy doesn't have another job, where are we supposed to go? And on top of that? We finally have a dresser for each of us!"

I know, the dresser comment was over the line, but after living for several years with only one dresser—I felt I needed to remind the Lord about it.

Plopping down in the middle of the floor, I watched my babies play. And the words in James sprang to my mind.

"Consider it pure joy, my brothers, whenever you face trials of many kinds . . . " Ouch. *Okay, so I haven't done a very good job in the joy department. All right, Lord. I will consider this joy.*

" . . . because you know that the testing of your faith develops perseverance." Double ouch. *My faith is weak, Lord. I've been questioning Your plan. I'm sorry. If You want us to take a step of faith, I'm willing—even if it means selling everything, (gulp!) including the dressers.*

As I continued to pour my heart out to the Lord, He gently pruned away my selfish thoughts and feelings until my heart was full of joy, faith, and a willingness to persevere. No matter what.

The very next day, God gave my husband a new ministry. And the blessings that poured out on us through that leap of faith are innumerable.

In the years that have followed, my joy has been severely tested. My son almost died, my daughter was diagnosed with an incredibly rare nerve disorder, medical bills soared with no hope of a cure on the horizon. And then, I watched as my child suffered for months on end, only to find out that we were dealing with another rare condition—one that required brain surgery.

"Perseverance must finish its work so that you may be mature and complete, not lacking anything." Those words ran to and fro in my mind as I watched my beautiful daughter sleep in the PICU after brain decompression surgery. I knew I wasn't finished. I definitely wasn't mature and complete. And I was okay with that. I would consider life joy, each trial, each test. Mature and complete would come one glorious day after perseverance here on earth.

My friend, if you are suffering in the trials of life, remember that God's joy is in the midst. Grab onto it.

"Consider it pure joy, my brothers, whenever you face trials of many kinds, because you know that the testing of your faith develops perseverance. Perseverance must finish its work so that you may be mature and complete, not lacking anything."

KIMBERLEY WOODHOUSE is a wife, mother, author, and musician with a quick wit and positive outlook despite difficult circumstances. A popular speaker, she's shared at more than six hundred venues across the country. Kimberley and her family's story have garnered national media attention for many years, but most recently her family was chosen for *ABC's Extreme Makeover: Home Edition*, *The Montel Williams Show*, and Discovery Health channel's *Mystery ER*, which premiered in 2008. Her story, *Welcome Home: Our Family's Journey to Extreme Joy*, releases in September 2009 from Focus on the Family. Kimberley lives, writes, and homeschools in Colorado with her husband and two children in their truly "extreme" home. www.kimberleywoodhouse.com

WHEN WE SURRENDER OUR PLANS
TO THE LORD'S PLANS, HE BLESSES US MORE
THAN WE COULD EVER IMAGINE

Ephesians 3:20 (NIV): Now to him who is able to do
immeasurably more than all we ask or imagine . . .

Sacrificed Dreams

When a business meeting was cancelled, I found myself with a free afternoon in Orlando, Florida. You'd think I'd be elated to have unexpected free time in America's beloved vacation destination, but for some reason I found myself feeling gloomy and depressed.

Then the realization hit me—it was the one-year anniversary of our heartbreaking miscarriage. It's hard to even say the word miscarriage; it paints such painful memories. My husband and I married in our late thirties and joyfully found ourselves pregnant in our forties. When we lost our baby, I felt as though I lost my one chance at being a mother. The memory hurt so deeply that I couldn't even go there in my mind.

To avoid the hurt, my thoughts wandered to a talk I was preparing for a women's Bible study on giving. I had been reading about sacrificial giving. As I wandered through a beautiful Orlando resort, I heard God speak to me. In a still small voice, in a way that only He can, the Lord whispered to me, *What about you? Are you willing to sacrifice?*

"What? Are You talking to me?" I silently questioned. *"Sacrifice what?"*

Then, plain as day, I felt a nudge from God. *Your dream of having a child,* God said.

Sacrifice my dream of having a child? I choked back tears.

Sacrifice my dream of having a child? I couldn't quite digest the thought. *How on earth could You ask such a thing?*

Running from the audacious thought, I quickly fled to my car and escaped to Downtown Disney. I glanced at the restaurants, but dinner alone with my thoughts didn't sound appealing.

Everywhere I looked young fathers twirled with darling daughters who were draped in princess costumes. Tourists were filled with joy in this magical place. All these happy people only served to illustrate that my own dream was unraveling. There I was in the middle of the happiest place on earth, and all I wanted to do was collapse in the middle of the street and cry.

I continued trying to drown out God's probing question about my willingness to sacrifice my baby dreams and headed back to the resort. Feeling depressed, I ordered a pizza.

As I ate away my pain, my hand reached for the television remote control. But God whispered to me again. *Stop running and spend some time with Me.*

Spend time with You? I didn't feel like doing anything with God, especially praying or reading the Bible! Yet, relenting, my hand dropped the remote.

For the next several hours I sat on the bed clinging to the hotel sheets, crying my eyes out as I duked it out with the Lord.

Am I willing to sacrifice? Sacrifice my biggest hope and dream?

Are you willing? He repeated.

"Am I willing to sacrifice having a family to do whatever You want me to do in my life? I can't believe You'd ask that of me." (Tears.) "You're the God who gives us the desires of our hearts. I love children. I'm great with kids, aren't I? Who am I if I'm not a mother?" (Sobs.)

My heart ached as I struggled to lay all my hopes and dreams at the feet of Jesus. I pleaded, "Other people have children, and they still do great things for You, God. Why can't I? Why do I have to sacrifice this dream?"

Are you willing? He persisted.

It took hours, but finally around midnight, disappointed and drained, I surrendered.

"Yes. I'm willing to sacrifice my dream. Why? Because You asked me to."

One month later . . .

A month went by and I began to experience some health issues. After several visits to the doctor, I was informed I was pregnant! *Me, pregnant? How could that be?* Repeated tests confirmed I was indeed pregnant.

Soon, I found myself visiting a prayer meeting where a guest speaker prayed individually for each person in the room. She had a special gift, knowing the prayer needs of the people without knowing the people themselves. After everyone in the room had been prayed for, I found myself standing before her.

She said, "You are pregnant, you're going to have a boy, your pregnancy won't be easy, but hang in there because you're going to have a boy and he's going to be fine."

The next several months were committed to prayer as we headed into a high-risk pregnancy. I was diagnosed with a rare blood condition that could be threatening to my life and the baby's. We had no health insurance, experienced the tragic death of my close cousin, and came face-to-face with two hurricanes.

Yet God met each of our needs in a miraculous way, and on December 1, 2005, we humbly welcomed a beautiful little towhead into the world, Luke Granger, naming him after Luke 1:37: "For nothing is impossible with God!"

My dear friend Criss said, "Maybe God just needed to know that you were willing to sacrifice your plans for His plans—that you trusted Him and His plan for your life. He needed to know your *heart,* and through surrender, He blessed you more than you could have ever 'asked or imagined.'"

....

KAREN GRANGER is a freelance publicist, writer, and keynote speaker for retreats and events. She is a columnist for the *Good News* in south Florida and enjoys writing inspirational stories for a variety of publications. She and her husband, Eric, live in south Florida with their son, Luke.

OUR LOVING HEAVENLY FATHER USES
LIFE'S DIFFICULT SITUATIONS TO MOLD US
INTO WOMEN WHO REFLECT THE
BEAUTY OF HIS CHARACTER

*Jeremiah 29:11 (ESV): For I know the plans I have for you,
declares the Lord, plans for welfare and not for evil,
to give you a future and a hope.*

Abandonment to Hope

It is my privilege to teach the students majoring in Home Economics-Family and Consumer Sciences at The Master's College. Before I started teaching at the college level, I taught Home Economics-Family and Consumer Sciences at the secondary level.

As we were growing up, my friends and I talked about many professions we might like to pursue—nurses, beauticians, and others. I always wanted to be a teacher. As a child I wanted to teach elementary school. When I started junior high I was scheduled for my first home economics class. I loved it and decided that I would like to teach home economics. I still have contact with the teacher who taught that class.

Early in my teaching ministry I was amazed to discover that my students thought my life had always been problem-free. One day a young woman walked into my office and bluntly stated, "I really don't know why I am here to talk with you. I have many personal problems and I *really* need someone to counsel with me. But since your life has always been so serene, I don't think you would understand!"

As she poured out her heart to me, it was as if I were looking in a mirror. Her life experiences were almost the same as mine. It was then I realized that I needed to share with my students that much of what I taught spiritually in the classroom was the result of the lessons I had learned about how God's grace covers my pain and transforms it into a beautiful pearl if I will allow Him to do so. Each difficult situation adds a new layer of nacre that increases the beauty of my seed pearl. It all began with . . .

Abandonment—the initial grain of sand

I was abandoned by my birth parents. When my mother left the hospital, I stayed.

During the first six months of my life, I battled pneumonia. Though I was unaware of my heavenly Father's presence, His promises to be a "father of the fatherless" and to provide "homes for those who are deserted" (Psalm 68:5–6) were functioning in my life. My abandonment was the tiny grain of sand that my gracious heavenly Father used to begin the process of transforming my life into a beautiful pearl.

Six months later I was adopted into a Christian family. At the age of ten, I learned in vacation Bible school that salvation was like being adopted into God's family. It was God's plan that the specialness of my first adoption would make me eager to become His daughter.

Reinforcement—the first layer of nacre

My church taught salvation each Sunday but did not teach me how to grow as His child. So *I* carried the burden of sick parents and many other problems, rather than casting my cares on Him (1 Peter 5:6–8). The death of my parents—my father when I was eighteen and my mother when I was twenty-three—applied the first layer of nacre to my seed pearl. The reinforcement layer made Hebrews 13:5–6, "I will never leave you nor forsake you," a reality in my life.

Growth—the second layer of nacre

My heavenly Father led me to Scott Memorial Baptist Church. There, I was confronted with my sin. My heavenly Father showed me through His Word that I must repent of the sin, trust in Jesus for salvation, and submit to Him as Lord (Romans 10:9). I agreed with His declaration that Jesus is Savior and Lord (Romans 10:10), and thus had my salvation confirmed (Romans 10:13). As I began to mature as a Christian, He applied the second layer of nacre to my pearl.

Reproduction—the third layer of nacre

From the date of that commitment, I have daily sought my heavenly Father's guidance. I desire to "walk by the Spirit" so I "will not gratify the desire of the flesh" (Galatians 5:16). I gladly responded to Him, as Mary did when she said, "Behold, I am the servant of the Lord; let it be to me according to your word" (Luke 1:38), by serving Him full-time in Christian higher education for the majority of my professional career. He knew I could serve Him most effectively as a single woman, and He has consistently provided for all of my spiritual, physical, and emotional needs (1 Corinthians 7:7–8; Philippians 4:19). On the day He welcomes me to my heavenly home, my pearl that began as a tiny grain of irritating sand will become one of polished perfection.

May I encourage you to record in a journal or notebook the layers of nacre God applies to your seed pearl? It is my prayer that your entries will remind you that the plans our gracious heavenly Father has for you will give you a future and a hope!

PAT ENNIS taught home economics for the San Diego Unified School District while developing the home economics department at Christian Heritage College. She moved to The Master's College in 1987 to establish the Home Economics-Family and Consumer Science Department that she currently chairs. Pat authored *Precious in the Sight of God: The Fine Art of Becoming a Godly Woman,* and coauthored *Becoming a Woman Who Pleases God: A Guide to Developing Your Biblical Potential, Designing a Lifestyle That Pleases God,* and *Practicing Hospitality: The Joy of Serving Others.*

SOMEBODY HAS TO
SET UP THE CHAIRS

Matthew 23:11–12 (NKJV): But he who is
greatest among you shall be your servant.
And whoever exalts himself will be humbled,
and he who humbles himself will be exalted.

Learning to Set Up Chairs

 Each December, as the New Year begins to peek over the horizon of promise, I spend time seeking the Lord for direction, asking Him some relatively simple questions:
* Do I continue along the same path?
* Should I look for a change of direction?
* How best can I prepare for what You want me to do, Lord?
And then I listen, eagerly anticipating the continued unfolding of His great plan and the part He desires for me to play in it.

In December 2005, however, I was not at all prepared for the seven-word directive that God whispered to my heart: *Somebody has to set up the chairs.*

Despite my initial confusion, I understood that God was calling me to a season of serving others. But isn't that what I was already doing? Hadn't I dedicated my life to writing and speaking the message of the gospel? What else could He possibly mean?

The more I thought and prayed about it, the more I knew I was supposed to make myself available to serve others in public ministry—which obviously meant I would have less time to continue developing my own public ministry, at least for that season. Admittedly, I arm-wrestled God for a short while on that part, but as always, He won, and I settled in for a time of serving others.

In addition, my mother (who was in her mideighties at the time and had already been living with us for a couple of years) needed more and more personal care and attention. Since I was her primary caretaker, that meant I now had to take care of things like making her bed, preparing her meals, taking her to the doctor or shopping—basically, anything she could no longer do herself. That, of course, meant even less time to devote to my own writing or speaking.

In the midst of all that, I caught myself one day in the midst of grumbling and complaining about never having enough time to devote to myself and my own needs. The sound of my own whining voice stopped me short, and I closed my eyes and asked God's forgiveness. In that instant I heard once again the words He had spoken to my heart a few months earlier: *Somebody has to set up the chairs.*

It wasn't until that moment that I realized my call to "set up chairs" was about more than serving others in public ministry. It was also about serving the people closest to me, right here in my own home. It was about daily laying down my life, giving up the right to plan my days and order my steps, so that I could help others fulfill the needs of their day—and to do so cheerfully and graciously. That's when I realized that without a continual, daily dependence on God's grace, I would fail, quickly sinking into a grumbling, complaining, me-first spirit.

"Help me, Lord," I prayed. "Give me the wisdom daily to know and remember that You have called me to do something that I simply cannot do in my own strength. Teach me, Father, to rely totally and completely on You—one day, one hour at a time."

Now that's a prayer God will readily answer! It is also an ongoing prayer, one I continue to utter often and earnestly. And each time God is faithful to answer.

As God called me to a season of "setting up chairs" for others, especially my dear mother, I began to learn much about gratitude and humility. Now, each time I find myself becoming impatient and irritable (and I certainly do at times!), I ask myself yet again which way

I will choose: His way or mine. Will I try to live this day putting myself first, doing everything in my own strength, making my own decisions and calling my own shots—or will I throw myself at His feet and admit that I am completely reliant on His grace to get me through, grateful for the opportunity to serve wherever He has called me?

Somebody has to set up the chairs.

God is still working in me to give me a servant's heart, but I have learned that it is only as I depend on Him that true love and humility will have its way in me. I have also come to understand that "setting up chairs" for others is indeed a joyous and honorable way to live.

KATHI MACIAS is a multi-award-winning writer who has authored twenty-six books and ghostwritten several others. A former newspaper columnist and string reporter, Kathi has taught creative and business writing in various venues and has been a guest on many radio and television programs. Kathi is a popular speaker at churches, women's clubs and retreats, and writers' conferences, and recently won the prestigious 2008 member of the year award from AWSA (Advanced Writers and Speakers Association) at the annual Golden Scrolls award banquet. Kathi "Easy Writer" Macias lives in California with her husband, Al, where the two of them spend their free time riding their Harley.

IN THE DANCE OF LIFE,
FOLLOW GOD'S LEAD

Psalm 30:11 (NLT): You have turned my mourning into joyful dancing. You have taken away my clothes of mourning and clothed me with joy.

Learning to Dance

 As a preschooler twirling around in dime-store pearls with a lopsided tiara and a pink tutu tied crooked around my waist, I felt certain I could save the world. While my dance teacher may not have agreed, she always smiled at me and said, "Brittney, what you lack in grace you certainly make up for in style." Taking that as a compliment, I smiled back, thinking that God had put a song in my heart and a dance in my soul that would never end.

At age five, that joyful song and dance came to an abrupt halt when my innocence was stolen through sexual abuse. This was the first time I began to wonder whether God had walked off the dance floor of my life, leaving me alone in a now shabby, torn tutu.

Six years later, I once again wondered where God was when I was diagnosed with Crohn's Disease, a chronic medical condition with no cure. Then, as a high school freshman, just when I was beginning to again hear God's song and believe I could trust Him enough to follow His lead, something happened that was so sudden, so devastating that I was certain God had turned His back on me.

On December 1, 1997, approximately thirty of my friends and classmates gathered in our school lobby in West Paducah, Kentucky, for a prayer circle that took place each morning before the start of classes. When the words "Amen" were spoken . . . BANG . . . a gunshot rang out from behind me! I saw my friend Nicole fall to the floor. She had been shot in the head. When I turned around, the shooter was just a few feet in front of me and I was staring straight down the barrel of a .22 caliber gun. Immediately shock set in and I froze as the gunman continued shooting everyone around me.

As blood from wounded classmates began to pool around my feet, another shot was fired and I felt a shove from behind. Within seconds I found myself huddled on the cold tile floor clutched in the arms of a friend who had just saved my life. With nowhere left to run, we laid flat on the floor watching helplessly as the gunman continued on his rampage. When the shooting finally ended, eight people had been critically shot, three of whom died, including my friend Nicole.

Devastated and angry at God for allowing so much pain, I began questioning everything I knew to be true. I wondered if God really loved me or if He was only tolerating me in order to stay true to His Word. The guilt and shame from my past were quickly becoming the validation I needed to treat myself as anything but holy. I felt completely abandoned with no hope God's presence would ever abide in me again. With every step, I was dancing my way into a song of self-destruction that would inevitably led to the depths of a pit I never could have imagined.

After years spent dwelling in a pit of self-destructiveness, I finally felt God's presence stirring in my soul while on an overseas medical missions trip. Amidst the brokenness of an impoverished Cambodian village, as I saw families forced to give up their children to an unknown fate, God ignited a passion in my heart for victims of human trafficking. I sensed God was calling me to become a bold advocate for women and children held captive in the world's fastest growing criminal industry: human trafficking.

Would I follow His lead? Doing so would require letting go of my anger toward God. Studying God's Word and counseling have helped me replace my anger at God with trust in God and His providence. It's an ongoing dance, with occasional rough patches, but He keeps reminding me of what's at stake—the lives of thousands (millions?) who wonder, as I once did, "Why doesn't God send someone to help me?"

God once seemed absent, but now, looking back and looking forward, I believe that He was and is always there on the dance floor of our lives, waiting for us to allow Him to transform our mourning into dancing.

BRITTNEY THOMAS is a popular public speaker among youth and adult audiences. Her tenacious spirit and faith in God has given her the opportunity to travel around the world boldly advocating for those without a voice. Brittney received her master's in public health in 2008 and currently lives in Lexington, Kentucky. You can contact Brittney through her website at http://lopsidedhalos .blogspot.com.

GOD'S TRUTH IS NOT LIKE MAN'S

Romans 8:31–34 (NIV): If God is for us, who can be against us? . . .
Who will bring any charge against those whom God has chosen?
It is God who justifies. Who is he that condemns?

I Just Don't Fit In

 Cliques are a part of our culture, whether we are in junior high school or the upper echelons of Manhattan society. We seem to have an inner need to belong and be deemed acceptable by our peers. Sometimes that means the right sneakers and sometimes it means invitations to the right party.

We desire to be known intimately, to be loved, accepted, and ultimately, found worthy. Unfortunately, the right designer brand does not lead to true acceptance. Human society is a fickle thing. As they say, "In fashion, one day you're in, the next day you're out."

My own story is about always being outside the circle, always looking in and assessing the situation, wondering if I might be found worthy to enter someday.

I grew up with a mentally retarded brother. My childhood was fraught with public humiliations and skin-crawling embarrassments. My brother was big, loud, and extroverted, and tended to invade people's space and spit as he talked, standing uncomfortably close to people as they tried politely to retain some personal space. Mine was that family other people stood back and pointed at, whispered about behind cupped hands, and generally just steered clear of, if at all possible.

The humiliation bore on me and I became leery of departing from home. Something as simple as a trip to the grocery store could invoke terror in me. *What might Gary say? Will he bother that cashier again? Does my mom have a lot to get? Will this take long?* I was expected to walk dutifully behind and not cause any trouble. I never told anyone it bothered me. Standing back, I was able to see in full view the looks of disgust, the wagging tongues and shaking heads while my mother simply tried to get as many groceries in the cart as possible while maneuvering Gary down the aisle—and hope there was no one else in the aisle; that would slow everything down.

Kids from school would sometimes come by our house and sit across the street, waiting for the "show" to start. On one such occasion, my brother came out of the house stark naked while my mother was filling up a baby pool in the front yard. *I could have died!* While my mother herded my brother back into the house, I stared at the kids across the street as they broke into uproarious laughter.

Fast-forward thirty-five years. I have my own four children now. One in particular tends to make public outings embarrassing. A few months ago, this child threw a violent tantrum in Target. While I tried to calm her and protect passers-by, I looked up and saw my other three children huddled off in the distance, humiliated and hoping to no one watching would connect them with us.

In their eyes, I saw myself all those years ago—the horror; the unsaid desire to disappear unnoticed; the self-induced separation. I stopped trying to calm my flailing child. I stood up and pulled her by the hand and walked out, letting the boys follow me behind at a distance. We got to the car and I looked at them all in the eye and apologized. Suddenly, I realized my mother never noticed the looks and the whispers because she was in the moment: loving my brother, doing what needed to be done.

My children do not humiliate me, simply because they are a part of me. While their behavior is sometimes unacceptable, *they* never are. That's what my mother taught me. Family is family—no matter what. When you love in this manner, you let go being concerned about the opinions and judgments of others. You cast off the lie that you are unacceptable or unworthy because of something you cannot control.

Maybe in your life, it's not that obvious. Maybe you feel unacceptable because you're in cheap jeans or live in the "wrong" neighborhood, or drive the "wrong" car.

People can be cruel. They can misunderstand, they can judge, they can gossip. But we are not responsible for them or their reactions to us. We are acceptable. We are only asked to obey in love, and His grace is sufficient. He is refining us, teaching us to be better versions of ourselves for the kingdom. In our pain, we learn to comfort another. And because of His grace, we belong. No team jacket required.

If you've forgotten you too are already a member of the only clique worthy of belonging to, here's your reminder:

"If God is for us, who can be against us? . . . Who will bring any charge against those whom God has chosen? It is God who justifies. Who is he that condemns?" (Romans 8:31–34).

KRISTIN BILLERBECK is the author of more than thirty books, a pioneer in Christian chick lit, and a lover of Jesus who feels eternally sixteen. She is a fourth-generation Californian who lives in the Silicon Valley with her husband and their four children.

GOD'S PATH FOR US
IS NOT ALWAYS EASY,
BUT IT IS ALWAYS BEST FOR US.

*Proverbs 3:5,6 (NIV): "Trust in the Lord with all your heart
and lean not on your own understanding; in all your ways
acknowledge him, and he will make your paths straight."*

To God Be the Glory

My husband, Randy, celebrated his (drumroll, please) fifty-sixth birthday recently. They call that a "belly button" birthday in Alcoholics Anonymous. Randy's sobriety birthday is coming up on eleven years—a miraculous, joyous occasion that has made the celebration of being another year older possible. Thanks be to God!

Yet this birthday was bittersweet. By age fifty-six, Randy could have retired from his job as an air traffic controller with a comfortable monthly income plus benefits. *Sigh* . . . In these tough economic times, that kind of financial security is hard to find. On those days when we struggle with the *could-have-beens*, Randy will say, "You know, we could have been retired now." We look at each other, roll our eyes, and manage to chuckle. Being able to laugh about our situation has been a long time coming, though.

Randy lost his job fourteen years ago, a devastating loss for him—and for me. It seemed like the end of the world, and it was . . . at least the end of our world as we knew it. But that's the toll of addiction. A bright and talented man, he had no power over alcohol. He had been through dozens of treatment programs, inpatient and outpatient, counseling, A.A., and other support groups. I believe all were helpful and moved Randy toward recovery, but he still hadn't reached the point of complete surrender even after losing his career.

I remember the heavy, almost palpable despair I felt. Fear's icy fingers threatened to strangle any hope I had. *God, how will I ever make it through all this pain and uncertainty? How will we make it financially?* My prayers sounded like a broken record. I memorized these words from Proverbs 3:5,6 out of necessity: "Trust in the Lord with all your heart and lean not on your own understanding; in all your ways acknowledge him, and he will make your paths straight."

When I look back, it is miraculous to see how the Lord stretched out a straight path in front of me. Not an *easy* path, but one that honored and pleased God. A path that was best for our family. I couldn't see where we were going, so all I could do was have faith for the next step. Sometimes the steps were tiny. Get out of bed. Take a shower. Get dressed. Take a walk. Fold the laundry. And most important, read God's Word. Then came larger steps: the decision to move to a small, rural community over the mountains, to trust God for provision for Randy and me, to believe there was still hope for healing and wholeness for us individually and as a couple. That's the essence of faith—walking to the very edge of what we know, what is familiar and tangible, and then having courage to take that next step into uncharted territory.

The journey toward sobriety for Randy, to ultimate freedom in Christ, though long and difficult, has left us with gratitude beyond words. These days we don't allow ourselves to wallow in self-pity. We both know we are blessed many times over. We realize alcoholism could have claimed Randy's life if he had continued drinking. My imagination has always been vivid in playing out worst-case scenarios that only by the grace of God never happened—the car accidents where Randy and/ or the other driver and passengers could have been killed or maimed, a prison sentence and unimaginable guilt that would have haunted us, or a tragic mistake on his job, bringing unimaginable suffering.

Sometimes God's grace comes in the form of hard lessons. Maybe it would have been nice to just hang out on our back deck on lazy summer days, sipping iced tea with no particular place to go. But having life, vibrant, busy with work and purpose is cause to celebrate. So when I brought out Randy's chocolate birthday cake with one bright candle (I was so sure I had a supply of those little birthday candles) and sang my solo rendition of *Happy birthday, dear Randy*, I meant it with all my heart.

. . . .

DEB KALMBACH is the coauthor of *Because I Said Forever: Embracing Hope in a Not-So-Perfect Marriage* and the author of a book for children, *Corey's Dad Drinks Too Much*. Her articles have appeared in *Focus on the Family*, *Moody*, *Christian Parenting Today*, and many other publications. She has been a guest on TV and radio programs and the cohost of a Seattle radio talk show. Deb and her husband, Randy, live in a tiny town in Eastern Washington. www.kalmbach.com

DISCOVER GOD'S PLANS

John 15:16–17 (NLT): You didn't choose me. I chose you. I appointed you to go and produce lasting fruit, so that the Father will give you whatever you ask for, using my name. This is my command: Love each other.

God's Plan . . . Not Mine

When I was twenty-two years old and pregnant with my third child, my friend from church told me she wanted to be a Christian writer. That struck a chord with me.

I loved to read, and before I became pregnant with my first child (as a seventeen-year-old high school senior), I'd done well in school. It was during that crisis pregnancy that I gave my life to Jesus. With this gift of salvation, I wanted more than anything to find a way to serve Jesus and to share His good news with others. Writing would be it!

I knew I was on the right track when I attended a Christian writers conference and I made my first sale. The article was titled *The Greatest Commandment, Part II*. It was about loving others as yourself—a concept I was trying to live out.

The next five years were busy as I raised kids, lived my married life, and wrote. Soon I was selling numerous articles a month—I was even chosen to write study notes for *The Women of Faith Study Bible*. Because I knew my life had purpose through writing, I was diligent about protecting my time. Then my pastor asked me to help start a crisis pregnancy center in our community.

It's not easy to flat-out say no to one's pastor. He knew about my teen pregnancy and the abortion I had at fifteen. He knew the years of heartache, sorrow, and regret. Instead of telling him outright I couldn't do it, I told him I'd pray about it.

The next morning I *did* pray. "God, You know I'm busy raising kids and writing. My words are going out all over the world. I'm already helping people."

What are you doing about those in your community? It wasn't an audible voice but rather a quiet thought that I knew wasn't from me. *How are you helping them?*

I knew God was asking me to put my writing on the back burner, but it was the last thing I wanted. I cried. I pouted. Launching a new ministry would take time away from *my* goals.

Reluctantly, I obeyed. I organized meetings to find volunteers, filled out the paperwork, and petitioned for financial support.

God opened many, many doors. And He not only showed up at the center, but in my heart. With each answered prayer for funds and volunteers, my sadness over my lost dreams was replaced by the excitement of experiencing God at work.

This realization hit home one day when I was working at the center. One of the visitors was a mom and her fifteen-year-old old daughter, Kayleigh, who'd just given birth.

"My baby's in intensive care," Kayleigh said. "But once she gets better, me and my boyfriend are going to get our own place." Kayleigh was young, wore pigtails, looked twelve, and had no clue about her challenges as a teen mom.

"We'd like to help where we can," I offered. I told Kayleigh about our young moms support group, and she showed up again and again.

When Kayleigh first started attending, she often distracted the others. She talked loudly, was rude, and bossed everyone around, even the leaders. I kept praying for God to change her heart. The thing was, God began to change mine. My love for Kayleigh grew.

Kayleigh had a second girl with her boyfriend. They still lived together, moving around with family and friends. Getting their own place had not happened.

One day I asked a simple question. "Kayleigh, why aren't you and Nathan married? You're both eighteen, and you have two kids. It's clear you're committed to each other."

Kayleigh looked surprised. "We don't have any money. I want a wedding and a white dress."

"Is that all?" The words spilled from my mouth before I had a chance to take them back. "We can give you a wedding."

And we did. The mentors provided the cake, flowers, and food. The day was perfect.

The next month Nathan and Kayleigh showed up at church. I was shocked to see them.

"Well, we couldn't come to church when we were living together," Kayleigh stated matter-of-factly.

I was pleased to see them there, but even more excited a few weeks later when they accepted Christ. Today, they are a dedicated Christian couple who share their hope found in Jesus with anyone who will listen. And that is just one young woman's story. In my heart there are many, many more stories tucked away and treasured.

When God made it clear that He wanted me to help young women facing crisis pregnancies, it wasn't about how successful I could become in life. Instead, God's plan was about what *He* wanted to do in the world around me.

Today, I am on the board of directors of Hope Pregnancy Center. I continue to mentor young mothers. I also still write . . . in fact, I have more projects than I ever hoped for or expected. Deep down inside I believe it's because I allowed God to mold an obedient heart. My community has been impacted . . . and the center has forever changed *me*.

"Here I am, God. Wherever You lead I'll follow." Wherever.

Are you choosing to ignore that little voice that tells you God has something else—something bigger than you can ever accomplish on your own?

TRICIA GOYER is the author of eighteen fiction and nonfiction books, including *Blue Like Play Dough*. She won Historical Novel of the Year in 2005 and 2006 (*Night Song* and *Dawn of a Thousand Nights*) from ACFW, and was honored with the Writer of the Year award from the Mt. Hermon Writers Conference in 2003. Tricia's book *Life Interrupted* was a finalist for the Gold Medallion in 2005. Tricia writes magazine articles for publications like *Today's Christian Woman* and *Focus on the Family*. Tricia also enjoys speaking. She and her family make their home in Montana.

THERE IS ALWAYS HOPE,
EVEN WHEN LIFE FEELS HOPELESS

*Romans 15:13 (NIV): May the God of hope fill you
with all joy and peace as you trust in him, so that you may overflow
with hope by the power of the Holy Spirit.*

Hope After Betrayal

 I thought I knew everything there was to know about my husband, Dave. I was eighteen when we first met and he was twenty. We dated for three years before we got married. Two beautiful girls, several pets, and a bunch of life decisions later, we had settled into a secure spot. Then after seventeen years of marriage, the house of cards fell.

The first card to drop was a call from a dear friend, who lived out of state. "Tim" bravely shared that he was stepping down as a deacon of his church. He was addicted to Internet pornography. I was taken off guard because this information didn't fit with all I knew about him. Tim was a loving husband and father. I tried to comfort his wife, "Sue," but had little to offer her. I could at least listen and try to understand her anger. Shaken by this news, I tried to talk about it with my husband, but he seemed to have little to say on the matter. A few weeks later I found out why.

Tim's confession caused my husband to realize he had the same problem. After a business trip, he confessed to me his struggles when he traveled. He went on to explain that pornography had been an ongoing battle for him since he was ten. Now I understood exactly how Sue felt. Everything I thought I knew about my husband felt tainted. The house of cards went down as I realized he had entered our marriage with a secret life. Thankfully, I knew whom to turn to and I called Sue. She was a comfort and a great resource but there was a lot of pain to sift through on my own.

I cried out to God, "Why?" I wanted to understand how this could happen. Sure that I had failed somehow as a wife, I felt hopeless. Divorce felt like an easy solution, but I didn't have a peace about it. I sensed it was too soon to make such a drastic decision, and also there were our daughters to consider. I continued to call out to God and ask, "Why in the world did this happen?" All the while, I reminded Him of the many ways I had tried to be a good wife and mother. God sent an answer, though as my sovereign Lord He certainly didn't owe me one.

A few days later after many tears and prayers, more details came out and my heart continued to break. My husband was crying and confessing that he felt like a failure and a monster. My eyes cleared and I saw Dave as a child, not a man—a child carrying around over thirty years of pain. Then I heard God's voice in my mind. The thought could not have come from me. *If you don't extend My grace to him now, he may never know it.* This answered my "whys."

In that moment I also realized God had not abandoned me. I had not married the wrong man. I had a responsibility to be Christ to my husband but I wasn't sure if I had the strength in me. Then with a power that was not my own, I put my arm around Dave. He wept.

He later said he expected me to kick him out or tell him off, but not to touch him with love. In that instant we were both changed. God had a plan for us even in our brokenness. I realized that everything I ever learned about Christ was true and not just sentiment. I had a better understanding of the cost of grace. Most of all, my hope was restored. I realized that as deep as the injury was, God was deeper still.

Much of my hope had been placed in my husband. Now it is firmly planted in the One who has walked with Dave to freedom from addiction and with me through the pain of betrayal. The journey has not been easy or quick, but God's faithfulness has been sure. My hope is built on nothing less than Jesus' blood and righteousness. Our marriage is no longer a house of cards.

It has been seven years since Dave's confession. God has built a new life for us. I now head up a ministry to wives of sexual addicts, and with Dave's assistance I've written a book titled *Hope After Betrayal.* We have a stronger marriage and family than I ever dreamed possible. By the grace of God, Dave and I have celebrated our twenty-fifth wedding anniversary.

....

MEG WILSON is an author and speaker with a heart for hurting women. After sifting through the rubble of her own past and pain, Meg loves to encourage others to reach out for the same hope she finds new in Christ every day.

SHAUNTI FELDHAHN

IN FINANCIAL TRIAL, BE FAITHFUL
AND TRUST THE ONE WHO PROMISES
TO PROVIDE WHAT YOU NEED

*Matthew 7:7–11 (NLT): Keep on asking, and you will receive
what you ask for. Keep on seeking, and you will find. Keep on knocking,
and the door will be opened to you. For everyone who asks, receives.
Everyone who seeks, finds. And to everyone who knocks, the door
will be opened. . . . If you sinful people know how to give good gifts
to your children, how much more will your heavenly Father
give good gifts to those who ask him.*

God's Generosity

 Our future looked bright. Newly married, with two graduate
degrees from Harvard, we left the ivory tower feeling secure and
confident in our earning ability and potential for success.

As we started our life together in New York City, Jeff and I often
heard the message "Trust in the Lord . . . cast all your cares on Him . . .
He will provide." And while we were grateful to believe in a God who
came to the rescue, "trouble" seemed a distant concept, especially in
terms of finances. Jeff and I had high-paying jobs; I was a Wall Street
analyst and he was a lawyer at a high-powered firm, and almost without
realizing it, we had developed a hefty dose of self-dependence.

I look back now and cringe at the times that I privately thought
about what a shame it was that with our earning potential we would
probably never fully understand true dependence on God. Oh, how

God must have chuckled at that one. And a loving heavenly Father knew much better than to let us continue down the road of self-reliance.

A storm was brewing. And then it poured . . .

We had moved to Atlanta to start a family. I began writing, which isn't very lucrative. So for the first time, we were completely dependent on my husband's salary.

Jeff started his Atlanta career at a law firm, but then his entrepreneurial heart jumped into high gear. So in 2000 he and some friends left their jobs, raised nine million dollars in capital, and invested all their efforts to start a technology venture. They worked very hard, but unbeknownst to them, the tech crash was looming around the corner.

Their company got hit hard. Jeff cut back his salary and eventually stopped taking a paycheck entirely in order to pay his workers. And then came the September 11 attacks. The company was forced to shut down operations. We were stunned, and left to face the devastation of massive loss. And instead of going back to a law firm full-time, Jeff felt strongly that the Lord was asking us to keep the company alive on life support until some distant day when it could be retooled and relaunched into a better market. But that meant that our family income would have to come from any part-time legal contract jobs he could bring in, and whatever consulting and writing income I could garner.

We embarked on a painful five-year journey when we had very little money coming in. What we did have was a new baby, a new mortgage, and a massive debt—we still had over $100,000 in student loans. For five years, we had no clue on Monday how we were going to pay the mortgage on Friday. We didn't know where we would get the money for food, fuel, or diapers.

But we learned. And in the process we learned true dependence on God. Every time we found ourselves slipping past the end of our ropes, God would provide. Help rarely came early. Instead, it was at the last possible moment when Jeff would get a new legal client, an anonymous check would show up in the mail, or our church would offer to cover our utility bills.

Going through this financial trial and lesson in trust was quite painful at first—but after a while it became an adventure. It showed us that God's Word is completely accurate. He is well aware of exactly what we need when we need it. As Jesus essentially put it, "If you sinful people want to and know how to give good gifts to your children, how much more will your perfect heavenly Father give good things to His children who ask!"

This message of God's generosity was so real to us that it became our main source of hope. It also became a challenge. It was very tempting to avoid tithing when there was so little coming in! But we knew we had to do it, even when we couldn't see how the budget was going to work. Now we realize that He gave us unexpected blessings because we practiced that discipline.

God explains this principle in Malachi 3:10: "Bring the whole tithe into the storehouse, that there may be food in my house. Test me in this, says the Lord Almighty, and see if I will not throw open the floodgates of heaven and pour out so much blessing that you will not have room enough for it."

Five years later, the floodgates opened for us. Rather suddenly, the idea came to us for the now bestselling books *For Women Only* and Jeff's companion book *For Men Only*. And I am convinced that the inspiration was a gift from God. Through it, He provided abundantly—both for our family and for the finances necessary for Jeff to relaunch his business.

. . . .

SHAUNTI FELDHAHN is the bestselling author of *For Women Only: What You Need to Know About the Inner Lives of Men* and the other books in the Only series. She holds a master's degree in public policy from Harvard University, has worked on Wall Street and Capitol Hill, and is a popular national speaker. More important, she is a wife to her husband, Jeff, a mom to two young children, and a daughter of the King who has learned that He is faithful in every trial.

SOMETIMES IT'S NOT UNTIL LATER
THAT WE SEE THE THINGS THAT
ARE GOOD FOR US

Romans 8:28 (NIV): And we know that
in all things God works for the good of those who love him,
who have been called according to his purpose.

Good for Me

 It's kind of weird that growing up in Hawaii, I didn't experience racism against me for the first half of my life.

Hawaii is comprised of mostly Asian or Pacific Islander ethnicities, so I grew up with friends who were Chinese, Filipino, Hawaiian, Korean, or Japanese American like I am. I had friends who were mixes of Asian and Caucasian ethnicities, and in general, I didn't notice race very much—I thought of my friend Kelli as the girl whose mom taught Spanish at the high school, and I thought of my friend Andrew as someone who joined the military like his dad.

But when I moved to California for college, I was suddenly surrounded by more Caucasians than I'd ever seen in my entire life. It was complete culture shock. I'd never met an Irish American, or Italian, or German, or Greek. I hadn't even realized the differences between the European cultures as they evolved in America.

I was also suddenly aware of racial tension. A second-generation Korean friend was uncomfortable with me because her parents still hated the Japanese. A Caucasian friend assumed I could speak Chinese, since I was Asian. An African American friend thought I was strange because I was completely clueless about the black culture and slang.

Instead of being just part of a faceless crowd, suddenly I was aware of my "Asian-ness." Suddenly I was aware of my "Japanese-ness." Suddenly I was aware of other people's ethnicities, whereas before I'd only noticed dark hair versus light hair, or blue versus brown eyes.

I was aware of more racial slurs said about me. I realized that some things I said in innocence were misconstrued. It became easier and safer to collect Asian friends around me, but then I was seen as being closed-minded and ethnocentric.

My college years were painful as I rediscovered my identity—as a girl, as an Asian American, as Japanese American, as female Japanese American, as a Christian female Asian American. I started to see how my parents' culture and my family dynamics had shaped who I was. I started to see how the church culture had also shaped my thinking, and how I'd shaped my thinking around the church culture—not always in good ways.

Then God encouraged me to pick up my writing again.

I'd laid it down for many years because God had wanted me to change my attitude. (I'd fought Him, but He'd won, naturally.) I'd been more interested in my name on a book cover than in writing for Him.

But years later, despite the fact I was now working in the biology research field, God told me I could start writing again.

I wasn't going to make the same mistake twice—"What do You want me to write about?"

"Write your heritage."

Those words were spoken over me in prayer by author Brandilyn Collins. She didn't know anything about me at the time, just that I'd started writing fiction. She didn't know about my college years, trying to get used to the new, suddenly Asian skin I found myself in, trying to understand what it meant to be a girl, a Christian, and Asian.

But God knew. And I think God brought me through that difficult time specifically so that I could now write "my heritage."

I changed the ethnically neutral heroine in my manuscript into a fourth-generation Japanese American girl who's Christian and has a completely whacked-out family. Suddenly she's dealing with issues like a nagging grandma, an annoying older brother who thinks he's Chow Yun Fat, and three special cousins who are closer to her than sisters because of their shared Christian faith in a family of predominantly Buddhists.

It felt great—not just the feeling that I was writing within God's will, but also writing this girl's story and taking tidbits I'd heard from friends or experienced myself. I realized how the stories I'd heard from my Asian friends about their families were similar to the stories I heard from other friends about their Irish, Italian, German, or Greek families.

God had taken that pain, that insecurity, that identity crisis, and made it into something fantastic in my writing. It's reassuring to know I'm writing with God's blessing, and it's fun writing about Asian American culture.

I challenge you to look at difficult things in a new light, to look at those experiences, and then to expect God to do something wonderful with them.

CAMY TANG writes romance with a kick of wasabi. Originally from Hawaii, she worked as a biologist for nine years, but now she writes full-time, is a staff worker for her church youth group, leads a worship team for Sunday service, and runs the Story Sensei fiction critique service, which specializes in book doctoring. On her blog, she gives away Christian novels and ponders frivolous things. Visit her website at www.camytang.com.

TRUST THE INTRICATE PERFECTION
OF GOD'S PLANS FOR YOU

*Jeremiah 29:11 (NIV): "For I know the plans I have for you,"
declares the Lord, "plans to prosper you and
not to harm you, plans to give you hope and a future."*

Releasing the Rope

On that rainy November morning, when the baby's heart stopped beating inside my womb, part of me died with her. In the next few months, I lost two *more* babies—and a bit of faith in God's goodness.

I tangled with Him, and others, from an ugly, hidden place in my heart. I fumed at thoughtless platitudes; grieved on my due dates; and clenched my teeth as women complained about children. When fertility treatments and surgeries failed me, I wondered if my Father had failed me, too.

"I just wish God's will could be the same as mine," I lamented to my sister.

"Shouldn't that be the other way around?" she questioned.

So I then fervently prayed that if God chose not to bless us with a baby, He'd teach me how to embrace His will.

More than anything in life, for *all* my life, I longed to be a mother. But all the while, God longed for me to trust Him—not just with little things or when His plans aligned with mine. I needed to stop this tug-of-war of wills, to trust Him with my heart's deepest longings, even when my logic begged otherwise.

Seasons passed. Slowly, Don and I accepted that we'd never again conceive . . . and later, that adoption agencies couldn't help us. Every door slammed shut, until we finally connected with an adoption attorney. When a birth mother chose *us* to parent her unborn baby, our hearts soared. And then plummeted just as low when she changed her mind.

We braced for disappointment when another birth mom chose us. As baby Peter's February due date neared, though, we found courage to hope again. When birth contractions began, we excitedly packed Peter's little "coming home" bag, called our families, and I resigned my position at work. Hours ticked by before the phone rang, bringing not the news I'd dared to expect, but the news I dreaded. I hung up and laid my head on the desk; I was too numb to even cry.

Don left on business the next day. I fled nearby to Lake Michigan's cold, windy shore to grieve privately and pray for God's solace. I was a "can-do, take-charge" girl. For five years, I had done everything in *my* power to have a child, and it wasn't enough. I had no more fight or hope. I had finally come to the end of myself.

And when I got there, God was patiently waiting.

That night as I lay broken and weeping, I felt God cradle me in His perfect peace. He instantly—completely—stilled my anger, struggling, and relentless questioning. He restored those parts of my spirit that had died—and had died to Him. He turned my grief to joy. Nestled in God's indescribable love, I, at last, hungered for Him and His will above all.

Six weeks after that midnight surrender, our lawyer called with a third adoption possibility. My heart and God's whisper said *no*. This time, I followed His leading. Every maternal instinct mourned when we turned down that baby. Don and I hung up the phone and wondered if we'd have another chance for a child. Meanwhile, God was revealing His impeccable timing and will.

For, that same day, our son David was born. When we held him, we knew *he* was the child God intended for us all along . . . just as *I* was becoming the trusting child my Father intended me to be all along.

When Don and I would lay in bed playing with David, we'd

jokingly ask God to send us another baby just like him, but in a "pink" version. Guess what? Eighteen months after David was born, his birth parents had another baby and placed her for adoption. They asked the attorney if we'd consider adopting her, to keep the siblings together.

Three days later, David had his sister; we had a daughter; and we glimpsed the intricate perfection of God's plans and love for us. Dave and Emmy, brother and sister in blood and spirit, are also best friends.

Twenty years later, I'd like to say I've never again played tug-of-war with God. What I *can* say is that I release the rope much sooner now. And when I do, in His own time, He once again reveals His perfect, impeccable plan.

CAROL KESNER RUHTER is passionate about helping women rediscover intimacy with God and with His creation. Her company, Trailbound Trips, offers women's weeklong hiking trips in such places as Maine's Acadia National Park and Montana's Glacier National Park. She also leads day-long hike and bike trips in Northern Illinois' wild places. A freelance writer and editor, Carol is currently collaborating with Marty Ramey on a devotional inspired by God's creation. She and Don live in suburban Chicago; Dave and Emily are now college-aged.

LEAN NOT UNTO THINE OWN UNDERSTANDING

Galatians 6:1, 4–5 (THE MESSAGE): Live creatively, friends . . .
Make a careful exploration of who you are and the work you have
been given, and then sink yourself into that. Don't be impressed with
yourself. Don't compare yourself with others. Each of you must take
responsibility for doing the creative best you can with your own life.

From a Marriage on the Rocks
to One Built on *The* Rock

Wayne and I married when I was still a teenager. My husband
was the breadwinner and decision maker. I was the stay-at-
home mother to our four children, all born within a five-year
span. Wayne, who worked as a construction electrician, paid the bills,
and I took care of the house and children.

My first exposure to the Bible came from a neighbor lady who invited
me to attend Bible Study Fellowship. It didn't take me long to realize my
need for Jesus Christ. Spiritually starved, I made my commitment to
Him in May of 1973 and Wayne accepted Christ shortly thereafter.

Our life together was good; we were on solid ground with each
other and with the Lord. In 1978 when I decided I wanted to write
books, Wayne was the first one to encourage me. In fact he was the one
who went out and rented that first typewriter on the rent-to-own plan.
He believed in me. He encouraged me, and when the rejections started
coming in, it was my husband who buoyed my spirits and comforted
me with the assurance that one day my books would sell.

Then—miracle of miracles—I sold that first book in September of 1982. My advance of four thousand dollars carried us through a bleak winter of unemployment. Construction was almost at a standstill, and Wayne and I were both grateful I was able to contribute for the first time to our family's income. Soon afterward I sold a second book and then a third. We were able to take our first real vacation in years. Wayne and I were both thrilled at my literary success.

Within a couple of years, my writing income was larger than the amount Wayne brought into our family. Within five I was paying more in income tax than he was earning.

Fissures in our marriage formed. Soon those small cracks became a huge, bottomless crevasse and we found ourselves in a constant battle of wills. I resented Wayne for making decisions without including me. He resented me making decisions on my own, especially in my career, without talking matters over with him. We both made mistakes; we were both stubborn and determined to have our own way. Instead of a cohesive unit we were continually at odds.

By 1988 it became apparent that we could no longer live together. Wayne moved out and frankly, I was glad to see him go. He traveled to another state and worked there. The release from the terrible tension in our household was instantaneous. We were better off without Wayne, I decided.

I hired my attorney. Wayne had his. I filed for the divorce first although Wayne agreed the marriage was over.

It didn't take long for the honeymoon period of life without Wayne to end. The children were hurting emotionally and mentally. I was too, although I was much too proud to admit it.

Then in church one Sunday, a visiting pastor mentioned the benefits of praying every day for an hour. Seeing how badly the children hurt because of the pending divorce, I decided if there was ever a time in my life when our family needed prayer, it was then. Every morning I got down on my knees and prayed for a solid hour. I did this for weeks. I didn't ask God to heal the marriage. By this time the divorce was days from being finalized; instead my prayers centered around the children and our lives together. I prayed God would heal Wayne from the pain this divorce had caused him and I asked God to bless my soon-to-be ex-husband in a number of specific ways.

A week before the divorce was to be finalized—a full year after Wayne had moved out—he contacted me. He was still living and working in another state. I was surprised to hear his voice as we had only been communicating through our attorneys.

"I don't want to do this," Wayne announced.

"You don't want the divorce?" I couldn't believe I'd heard him correctly. Wayne was the one who'd moved out and moved on.

"Frankly, the divorce isn't working for me."

This wasn't an answer to my prayers. I had put the marriage behind me. We had tried so many times before and it had failed. I didn't believe another attempt to live together would change anything.

In the end, we compromised. Wayne moved back to the area and rented an apartment. Then we dated for six months before we made the decision for him to return to the family home. When he did move back in, my husband stated that this new commitment had to be forever, otherwise the threat of divorce could become a revolving door. I saw the wisdom of his words.

This year Wayne and I will celebrate our fortieth wedding anniversary.

God took the mess we had made of our marriage. He took the pain, the resentment, and anger. Next He sent us both our separate ways while He worked on our hearts. The grain of sand was our faith in Him, which neither of us had abandoned. God worked all the negative emotions and through prayer, forgiveness, and an abundance of love, He gave back to Wayne and me the pearl of a solid, loving marriage.

With more than sixty million copies of her books sold, *New York Times* bestselling author **DEBBIE MACOMBER** is a leading voice in women's fiction worldwide. The Washington native and mother of four grown children is known for her heartwarming stories about small-town life, home and family values, women who knit, and enduring friendships. The author of the nonfiction book *Knit Together: Discover God's Pattern for Your Life*, Debbie serves on the national advisory board for *Guideposts* magazine. She and Wayne, her beloved husband of forty years, winter in Vero Beach, Florida.

GOD NEVER WASTES OUR PAIN

2 Corinthians 4:16–18 (NASB): Therefore we do not lose heart,
but though our outer man is decaying, yet our inner man is being renewed
day by day. For momentary, light affliction is producing for us an eternal weight
of glory far beyond comparison, while we look not at the things which are
seen, but at the things which are not seen; for the things which are seen are
temporal, but the things which are not seen are eternal.

The Treasure in Our Suffering

 One morning in May, I was taking a brisk walk. Halfway through the walk, I was struck with intense pain and knew I had another bladder infection. I also knew that once I got home, soaked in a hot tub, and got on antibiotics, the pain would go away as it had the other times.

But this time, the pain did not go away. It continued for three years. During those years I had to drastically change my lifestyle. I could not remain standing for more than a few minutes without feeling pain. My ministry as a missionary in a small French church was greatly limited. Just venturing outside the house was sometimes an ordeal.

Pain got my attention. Quite often, all I could do was lie in bed with a hot water bottle. Sometimes I prayed. Sometimes I cried. My journal became the place where I'd pour out my heart to God with questions and praise. Here are a few things I began to see:

The Word of God is a solid rock to minister comfort and healing and hope. God's Word became real and practical to me. That familiar verse in Matthew 6 became my mainstay. "Do not be anxious for tomorrow, for tomorrow will care for itself. Each day has enough trouble of its own." And He was always there for me, to give me the strength for that one day.

I began studying verses on suffering, verses I knew, but had not really applied to my life. It struck me in a new way that the Bible does not say *if* you suffer or experience trails but *when* you experience them. Pain, whether physical, emotional, or spiritual, is part of the human experience.

James says, "Consider it all joy *when* you encounter various trials . . ." How could I experience joy when I was in agony? The verse goes on: " . . . knowing that the testing of your faith produces endurance and let endurance have its perfect result that you may be perfect and complete, lacking in nothing." According to the verse, joy comes because I know and trust that God is using this trial to make me more like Him. Trials are often God's means for forming our character so that we can become more like Christ.

I was encouraged by friends acquainted with suffering to ask the question, "What is it, God, that You want me to learn through this trial?" One dear friend sent me a poem called "Don't Waste the Pain" and that became my prayer. "Lord, don't let me waste this pain."

All of a sudden my priorities became extremely clear. No longer did I feel guilty about not being able to do everything others asked of me. I knew my limitations all too well. I began to discover the freedom in pain. Pain called me to God and made me completely dependent on Him. I didn't know why I had to endure this pain, but God met me in my suffering—through prayer, listening to praise music, or just crying out to Him in desperation. He sent people my way—a lesson in humility for me, the missionary, to let others minister to me.

My faith was tested each day, and I came up against this: Either God is on the throne or He isn't. I believe God is in complete control of my life and of this world. On some days it felt like more than I could handle, but years of walking with God had taught me to hang on to what I knew was true. I felt like my life was completely out of control. But He would often remind me that He was in perfect control. He was not surprised or overwhelmed by my circumstances. This knowledge brought peace.

Suffering makes the promise of heaven so much more real. No more pain! And Paul tells us that our suffering serves the purpose of helping us comfort others in their afflictions. So many people confided in me simply because they knew I lived with chronic pain. I didn't have answers, but I listened and cared, which was often what they needed most.

In the midst of this unanswered prayer for healing, the Lord was answering many other prayers and using this trial for my good and His glory. There was not a lot of room for pride when I saw God using me in spite of my illness. On my own strength I struggled, questioned, got angry. But when I allowed God's Spirit to work in me so that I responded with hope and joy and peace in spite of my illness, this encouraged others and pushed me along in my Christian walk.

God was alive and at work in my weakness. There was a lot less I had to offer Him so I had to accept His love for me just as I was. Why is that so hard for us to do?

Pain taught me how precious life is. Even with chronic pain, each day held many moments of joy, and I paid attention to those moments:

ELIZABETH MUSSER, a native of Atlanta, Georgia, now living in Lyon, France, is a novelist who writes what she calls "entertainment with a soul." Her novels have been acclaimed in the United States and in Europe. Elizabeth's new novel, *Words Unspoken*, will be released in May 2009. For over twenty years, Elizabeth and her husband, Paul, have been involved in missions work with International Teams. The Mussers have two sons. To learn more about Elizabeth and her books, please visit her website at www.elizabethmusser.com.

A bright bed of flowers, a vibrant blue sky, a warm hug from my children, a kind gesture from my husband, a note of encouragement from a friend, a pain-free hour. God showed me the beauty of simplicity as I was forced to slow down. And as I practiced praising God in the midst of the pain, something amazing and amazingly simple happened: He gave me the strength to carry on.

That season of pain helped me see more of Jesus, understand more of His love for me, trust Him more, and learn a little bit more about how to have joy and praise in hard times. I truly believe that God never wastes the pain in our lives.

NOBODY'S PERFECT—BUT JESUS IS—
AND THAT'S ENOUGH

2 Corinthians 12:9 (NIV): But [God] said to me, "My grace is
sufficient for you, for my power is made perfect in weakness."
Therefore I will boast all the more gladly about my weaknesses,
so that Christ's power may rest on me.

Future Perfect—Who, Me?

My mother called it my sloppy stage. Most little girls experience ponytail meltdown after rowdy recesses of jumping rope, hanging from monkey bars, and playing tackle with the boys. My classmates Suzy and Laura and I only checked the restroom mirror if we needed Band-Aids on our noses. Sometime during fifth grade, however, my girlfriends got it together and made the mirror their permanent address.

But my sloppy stage never ended. For me, kneesocks existed in name only; mine slid into fat clumps of wrinkles around my skinny ankles. My carefree skirt zippers wandered around my waistline at will. I wore spaghetti sauce on my ears, even when I hadn't eaten spaghetti for a week.

Adolescence brought scary new variations on the theme. Pantyhose had not yet hit the market, so garter belts presented a mystery even more complicated than algebra. I wasn't sure which garter to fasten where, and they made me walk funny. Sometimes the garters worked loose, snapping at my legs like slingshots.

Over the years, when even bribes and threats failed to produce recognizable school pictures, my mom began to suspect a genetic defect. She did her best to help me battle my handicap, but, as an adult, I still struggle with collars that crumple, rumple, and collapse. I attract lint balls as if my wardrobe were made of Velcro. I also remain a reluctant lifetime member of the Jungle Mouth Club. Our credo: the amount of stringy spinach stuck between front teeth is in direct proportion to the status of the person we want to impress.

Throughout the decades, I've longed to be one of those people whose labels never stick out, whose purse straps cling discreetly to their arms instead of grabbing every doorknob they pass. I've tried not to give up hope. But recently, I arrived at an important conference networking session carrying a briefcase to complement my power suit, matching shoes—and a bright-colored Chiquita banana sticker on my bottom.

It's official: I give up! Perhaps I'm finally learning what God wanted me to discover the first time strained spinach hung from my one and only tooth: He loves me as I am. According to the Bible, God keeps count of every hair on my head—but it doesn't say they all have to stay in place. He used Deborah, Israel's judge, who must have missed her standing beauty appointment while camping out with soldiers as they fought God's enemies. He carried on an extra close relationship with Anna, who spent so many years in prayer that she probably lost track of the latest trends. Most important, God's Son was born to a poor teenager who probably hadn't bothered to accessorize when shepherds showed up to worship Him.

When I read in God's pages that He looks on the inside, not the out, and accepts the messy, wrinkled love of less-than-perfect people, it made me want to grab the hem of His pure, perfect robe and hang on forever. Especially when He says one day He will give me one just like it—and I'll never have to carry stain stick in my purse again. In heaven, I will be perfect. Perfect!

As I read more in His Word, however, I discovered a truth that shocked me down to my bunchy socks: God not only loves those on the Most-Likely-to-Wear-Produce-Labels list, He also loves women like

132

Esther, a ravishing, diplomatic beauty queen, and Sarah, the siren of the Old Testament. And He loves Suzy and Laura and other got-it-together types. The more I read, the more I realized God sees the dirty faces and hearts we all hide. How He longs to give all His daughters extreme inner makeovers so we can accept ourselves and each other!

With His help, I slowly am learning to accept the flawless and faultless. When one starts to fix her already perfect face and hair in an airport restroom mirror, I make a conscious effort not to scoot to the other end. And when I spot a fashion model lookalike at a party, I don't run screaming for cover. Now I actually enjoy friendship with the petite blonde cheerleading coach who rescued me from the Chiquita banana sticker.

I could ROFLOL with her, because she and I are sisters in the Lord.

And we're both future perfect.

RACHAEL PHILLIPS keeps busy writing in the second-story many-windowed office she has dubbed the "Tree House," a fulfillment of her childhood fantasy. She has published humorous magazine articles in *Virtue, Today's Christian Woman,* and *Marriage Partnership.* Her novel *Song of the Orphan Train* won first place in the Young Adult category of the 2007 ACFW Genesis Contest for unpublished fiction. Three of her humorous stories are in *Help, I Can't Stop Laughing!* Rachael has also authored four biographies and *Well with My Soul,* a collection of four mini-biographies of hymn writers. Rachael and her husband, Steve, a family physician, have three grown children and two grandchildren.

YOU CAN'T HELP WHAT HAPPENS
TO YOU IN LIFE, BUT YOU CAN
CHOOSE YOUR RESPONSE

Matthew 28:20 (NRSV): And remember,
I am with you always, to the end of the age.

God Stayed with Me

 June 28, 2004 started out like most Monday mornings in our house. I went to our daughter Virginia's room and said, "I thought you were going to get up at six, and it's now six thirty." I usually make her sit up and hug me, but we didn't get home until after ten the night before and I knew she was tired. I went back to my room and started to get in the shower.

I called back to Virginia's room. "Virginia, are you up?"

She replied with, "I'm getting dressed, Mom."

My husband had a big project that he was working on and went on to work. After I got out of the shower, I called back to Virginia and asked how she was doing. After asking a few times, I went to her room and she was lying on her bed dressed with her feet on the floor and one shoe on.

I stood in the doorway and said, "Virginia, get up honey, you fell back asleep. It's almost seven and we need to catch the bus in a few minutes."

When she didn't respond I went over to her; her eyes were almost closed, her lips were blue, and she wasn't breathing. I called 911. I just knew it was a heart problem and that the paramedics could come and revive her and we would go to Children's Hospital, find out what the problem was, and get it fixed.

The paramedics were at the house in less than ten minutes. They checked for a pulse, said, "she's down," and asked me to leave the room. The police told me not to worry, that they would lock up my house and I could ride in the ambulance. I kept praying for the paramedics to get her heart started as I called family members to meet me at the emergency room.

A roomful of people were waiting for Virginia in the ER. A nurse ushered me into the room next to the trauma room and a chaplain came in and we prayed. A doctor came in and by that time, my husband, sister-in-law, and a few coworkers had arrived. The doctor said that they had gotten her heart started in the ambulance, and we would be headed up to the ICU soon. I was so relieved; my baby was going to live, and God had answered my prayers that they had gotten her heart started. Her dad arrived and I shared the wonderful news with him. Then the doctor was summoned back into the trauma room because Virginia was crashing. More prayers. . . . They came back and said that they couldn't get her to respond and in a last-ditch effort, her dad and I went in and held her hand and talked to her and begged her to come back, but . . . she was gone. By now, it was only 8:00 in the morning, but it had been the longest hour of my life.

The doctors told me they were sorry, but they didn't know what happened. We would have to wait for the autopsy results, which could take a few days. We stayed in the room with her and I kept begging her to start breathing again, but it wasn't going to happen. By now, I was begging God for a miracle. The pastors from my church arrived and her father and I each held her hand as we prayed. We only had to wait until late in the afternoon to learn that Virginia's heart was fine, but she had an aneurysm deep in her brain that ruptured and took her immediately.

We decided to have the funeral on Wednesday afternoon, and to make it a Witness to the Resurrection that would be a tribute to the wonderfully kindhearted child God had given to me for eleven short years.

The day of the funeral came and I kept hoping that I was going to wake up from the nightmare of the past two days. However, it was real and we had to proceed. As I walked into the sanctuary, I felt a growing anxiety. I didn't want to say good-bye to the daughter I loved more than life itself and who had brought so much joy into my life. I just wanted to scream and run from the room. I didn't see how I could make it through the next forty-five minutes.

But at that point, a sense of calm descended upon me. It was as though God wrapped me in His arms and told me that He would see me through this. It was the most amazing feeling, and I was able to give my daughter the final good-bye that she deserved. I was also concerned about John, her sixteen-year-old brother. John did a wonderful job reading from Psalm 27, and I was proud of the courage and strength he showed in speaking in front of six hundred people.

A few days after the funeral, I was talking with a friend of mine; she wanted to tell me about her experience at the funeral. She described how, as she saw me walk into the sanctuary, she was filled with anxiety and dread. However, a sense of calm came over her and her anxiety went away. I truly believe that God not only took me in His arms, but He took her also.

As I have taken this journey of grief, I am reminded that God is with me. And I have been blessed by goodness and mercy from many people. I do not understand why my precious Virginia died or, for that matter, why any child dies, but I have faith in God's plan for my life, and faith is a very powerful force. I know that one day we will be reunited.

I wrote a letter that was read at the funeral, which ended with this quote from Romans 5:

"We also boast in our sufferings, knowing that suffering produces endurance, and endurance produces character, and character produces hope, and hope does not disappoint us, because God's love has been poured into our hearts through the Holy Spirit that has been given to us."

Dedicated in loving memory of Virginia Talbot Markle

MELANIE TALBOT MONTGOMERY lives in Birmingham, Alabama, and is the director of administrative and fiscal services for the UAB School of Health Professions. Her son, John Markle, is a student at the University of Alabama. She enjoys traveling, reading, and spending time with friends and family.

LISTEN FOR THE "UNFORCED RHYTHMS" OF GOD'S GRACE

Matthew 11:28–29 (THE MESSAGE): Are you tired? Worn out?
Burned out on religion? Come to me. Get away with me and
you'll recover your life. I'll show you how to take a real rest.
Walk with me and work with me — watch how I do it.
Learn the unforced rhythms of grace.

My Capsized Life

I married a tenacious man.

From our first meeting it was clear that he desired nothing more in life than to be a warrior for the King and His kingdom. I admired his resiliency and determination. With high hopes for our future together, Ross and I began serving side by side in youth ministry.

Seventeen years into our journey, our family, which now included a young son and daughter, went through a shipwreck season that lasted and lasted and lasted. We already had weathered the usual string of life storms, but this time the waves kept coming. All four of us moved in with my parents, where we shared a basement room with the washer and dryer. We lived there for six months before a new ministry opportunity opened up.

Packing our gypsy amount of belongings in our van, we moved to another state, eager to enter a new season. I was ready to be "home." But only a few months later the next wave hit. Ross's mom went into a diabetic coma and passed away. We spent a week in California for her funeral, but when we returned home, we were told that the church leaders had met while we were gone and decided to let Ross go from his position. No clear reason was given. The dismissal was awkward and pretty awful.

Usually when you lose a loved one or lose a job, you turn to your church family for support. However, when you lose a loved one, a job, *and* your new church family all within a few weeks, well, the shock carries you for just so long. Then you start asking each other the unanswerable questions over and over: What did we do wrong? What should we do now? What are we going to do?

My tenacious husband took the first job he could get, working construction. He heard about a new church starting up at a nearby school and decided we should attend.

On that restart Sunday morning, I managed to get myself and the kids up and dressed. But then it happened. I snapped. When Ross was ready to walk out the door for church, he couldn't find me. I had crawled into the back corner of our closet and was curled up in a wailing ball, rocking back and forth.

"I can't," I sobbed. "I can't."

At my request Ross took the kids to church and left me to decompress alone. But I wasn't alone. The Lord was near. So near. He said He's near to the brokenhearted, and I certainly qualified. I told God I still liked Him. I loved Him, actually. That hadn't changed. The problem was His children. I didn't like them anymore. I didn't like the way they'd treated my family and me.

I wasn't tenacious and resilient like my husband. I was broken. Had God forgotten that I'd promised long ago to serve Him *whole*heartedly? Not *broken*heartedly.

All I could do that particular Sabbath was breathe. It was that steady sort of ebb-and-flow breathing, the kind where you are quiet enough to hear your breath and feel your heart and realize you are at God's mercy for each exhale and each pulse. He is God. This is His arrangement; this mysterious pattern of receiving and giving, of filling and releasing. This is how He rules the seas of life. He gives and He takes away.

Yes, my life had capsized. But I was being carried along on the unforced rhythm of God's grace.

Eventually I washed up onshore, tattered but still breathing. I stood up, walked around, ate, slept, gave my children kisses, offered my husband smiles. I drew near to God. Closer and closer, and just as He promised, I began to recover my life. Soon I joined my husband and children at the new church. There, in the midst of a bunch of God's people, my broken heart mended.

If you find yourself among the brokenhearted as you read this, God is very near to you. His invitation stands:

"Are you tired? Worn out? Burned out on religion? Come to me. Get away with me and you'll recover your life. I'll show you now to take a real rest. Walk with me and work with me—watch how I do it. Learn the unforced rhythms of grace."

ROBIN JONES GUNN is a frequent speaker locally and internationally. One of her favorite topics is how God is the Relentless Lover and we are His first love. She delights in telling stories of how God uses fiction to change lives. She also serves on the board of directors for Media Associates International and the board of directors for Jerry Jenkins' Christian Writers Guild. She and her husband, Ross, currently live near Portland, Oregon. They spent their first twenty-two years of marriage working together in youth ministry, and enjoying life with their son and daughter, who are now both grown.

JESUS CAME FOR THE LEAST OF US

*Mark 10:14 (NIV): Let the little children come to me,
and do not hinder them, for the kingdom
of God belongs to such as these.*

Marissa and the Bear
(A Letter from Migrant Camp)

Dear Marissa,
    I remember you there with your big brown eyes—eyes that could melt a hundred hearts. I remember looking into those deep pools of brown and wondering what you were thinking, and what you were feeling, and not being sure that I had the right words to ask you. I remember holding your hand and walking outside the chapel door. It was cold—bone-chilling cold. I had on a long-sleeved shirt and a sweatshirt. You were dressed in only a short-sleeved shirt. You had a sweater, but you put your sweater around your teddy bear, wrapping him up like an infant. Miss Brenda and I both tried to persuade you to put the sweater on yourself, but you would not. You were determined to care for the little bear entrusted to you.

    If ever I decide to be a bear, I hope that I am yours. You are a good mother of teddy bears.

    I wondered as I watched you caring for the bear so quietly and so meticulously. I wondered if anyone ever cared for you that way. Did anyone ever wrap you in a warm sweater when you were cold? Did anyone ever hold you tenderly and sing you little songs? Did anyone ever put your needs before their own?

You couldn't tell your story. It was too scary, too hard, too much. You only sat and held the bear and occasionally looked at us with those big, brown eyes. We learned your story from your church leader:

Once upon a time, there was a little girl who was a part of a migrant family. She had big, beautiful brown eyes that sparkled and shone when she smiled. She had a father and a mother who were supposed to care for her, and love her, and protect her—that's your job when you are a father or a mother. Her father didn't take care of her, though. He came into her room and hurt her. He hurt more than just her small body; he hurt her heart. The man that she trusted and loved, betrayed her. Mothers are supposed to protect their children, but Marissa's mother did not protect her. She did not even believe her when Marissa told her what had happened.

So, the little girl with the big brown eyes doesn't talk much. Her eyes don't sparkle and shine anymore, and her smiles are rare. And no one lived happily ever.

I wanted the story to not be true, Marissa. I wanted it to just be a fairy tale . . . but it wasn't. Even though your mother believes you made it up, sadly, this is a true story. And the end of the story hasn't been written yet. I wonder how the story will end, Marissa. Will you live happily ever after? Will anyone ever care for you like you are caring for your bear? Will the hurt in your heart ever be healed?

We finished talking—you, Miss Brenda, the bear, and I. I said, "Marissa, do you have any idea how special you are to God?" You shook your head no. I tried to tell you. I tried to tell you with all the words I knew. I tried to say how very special and important you are. I wanted to say more, but there wasn't time.

I am home now, Marissa. I am sitting in my house, looking at my Christmas tree, and thinking—thinking about you. Slowly, I think I am beginning to understand. You, Marissa, have been my teacher—you and the bear. You are why the Christ child came. You are why Christmas happened. It's because there is a God who loves little girls who only have teddy bears to talk to—that's why Jesus came. He came because He wanted to offer you Someone else to talk to—Someone who could listen even better than the bear. He came to offer you Himself, Marissa. He came because He made you with big brown eyes that smile and sparkle, again.

I bought a small bear today. I hung it on my Christmas tree, even though it doesn't match anything else. I hung it there to remind me of you, Marissa. I hung it there to remind me of who Jesus came for—He came for the lost, the forgotten, those who have no protector, those who have no one to wrap them in a warm sweater and keep them safe—that's why Jesus came.

SHARON THOMPSON RHEA enjoys writing, teaching, counseling children, and building bridges of compassion to forgotten people. She serves as international projects coordinator and family camp director for WinShape Foundation. A licensed school psychologist and passionate power lifter, she holds a PhD in educational psychology and a master's degree in counseling. Sharon has served orphans and the poor in forty-seven countries, most recently in Ethiopia and China. She has taught graduate psychology and penned advice columns for students. Sharon and her husband, Claude, reside in the Atlanta area.

GOD IS RIGHT ON TIME

*Psalm 37:4 (NIV): Delight yourself in the Lord
and he will give you the desires of your heart.*

Waiting and Delighting

 Waiting is not my forte . . . neither is not knowing how things are going to turn out. When I was trying to get my first book published, I was forced to address both conditions.

I shouldn't be a writer. My degree is in architecture. I've never had a writing course. In truth, I started by trying to get a secular novel published. But God had other plans, and after many missteps I was led to write a Christian novel. I felt I was on the right road. God's road. And the writing of this first novel for Him directly corresponded to a renewing of the faith of my youth. I was fervent for the Lord, yet I had much to learn about faith. And much to hope for. When I sent out a synopsis and a few chapters of this first novel, I was just sure it would get a yes immediately.

I received rejections. *Hmm.* This wasn't how it was supposed to work. Psalm 37:4 said if I delighted in the Lord, He would give me the desires of my heart—and my heart longed to get a novel published.

Eventually a publisher did call and wanted to see the entire manuscript. Finally! Surely, now it would happen!

I waited for them to call and gush about its magnificence.

And waited.

163

And waited. The usual wait-time to get a response was eight to twelve weeks. But when I hadn't heard anything at fifteen weeks, sixteen . . .

One day when I was lying down for a nap, I prayed, "Lord, when will I get a yes on my book?" I fell asleep and had a vivid dream. I looked down on the couch, but it was empty but for a throw pillow at either end. Suddenly, a light shown down on one of the pillows and revealed the number "15". I immediately woke up and remembered my question: "When will I get a yes on my book?"

The fifteenth!

On the fifteenth, I took the phone with me everywhere, ready for the call. Nothing happened. I was disappointed, and yet . . . God had not said which fifteenth! The next month on the fifteenth, I would get a yes.

But I didn't. So much for my message from God.

The months passed. A year passed . . . the publisher encouraged me with phone calls but they weren't ready to commit. I thought about withdrawing it and sending it somewhere else. But I didn't. Somehow I knew this was the right place for the book.

While I waited I was not stagnant. I started another book. I read the Bible through. I went to church. I listened to Christian radio. And I prayed—prayed every which way: standing, sitting, on my face; whispering, shouting, crying, pleading . . .

One day I came to a crossroads and wrote in my prayer journal:

In the intro passage to 2 Samuel, it says, "We may not understand why God seems to move slowly at times, but we must trust him and be faithful with what he has given us." This was in reference to David becoming king but having to wait for many years. If I may be so bold as to apply this to my situation, Lord . . . I have not been anointed to be king by a great prophet like Samuel, but in my heart, I have received a promise from You that my book will be published and will reach many people. Even as I beg for it to be accepted today, I will wait longer, Lord, years if necessary. You are preparing its way in order that it may bring You glory. I don't want the glory, Lord. Not anymore. It scares me. I just want the book to be out there, doing something, instead of lying dormant. I want to share it, Lord. Please let me share it soon!

Three days later, I got a yes.

God's timetable is different than ours—He is never late and never early. Waiting was essential to my spiritual life; God needed me to grow. He couldn't give me a yes when I wasn't ready.

I *was* a little disappointed the *yes* didn't happen on the fifteenth of the month. And yet . . . I soon realized it had been exactly fifteen *months* since I'd first received the phone call from the publisher asking for the manuscript. How wise God was *not* to have shown me "15 months" on that pillow! I would have given up. And yet, the fifteen months God made me wait allowed me to learn about Him, learn how to pray, learn how to trust. And during that time He changed the desire of the heart to match His.

So what are the desires of your heart? Delight in the Lord and see how He makes them materialize in His perfect way. God gives us "immeasurably more than all we ask or imagine" for His glory! (Ephesians 3:20)

. . . .

NANCY MOSER is the author of three inspirational humor books and eighteen novels, including *Mozart's Sister, Just Jane,* and *Time Lottery,* a Christy Award winner. She is an inspirational speaker and gives seminars around the country. She has earned a degree in architecture; run a business with her husband; traveled extensively in Europe; and has performed in various theaters, symphonies, and choirs. She and her husband have three grown children and make their home in the Midwest. Read more about her books at www.nancymoser.com.

CAREGIVING SPEEDS THE
PROCESS OF PEARL MAKING

2 Corinthians 1:3–5 (NIV): Praise be to the God and Father of our Lord Jesus Christ, the Father of compassion and the God of all comfort, who comforts us in all our troubles, so that we can comfort those in any trouble with the comfort we ourselves have received from God. For just as the sufferings of Christ flow over into our lives, so also through Christ our comfort overflows.

Pain Forms Pearls

 Although I'm only twenty-three, I already possess enough pearls for a necklace!

Pain visits my home frequently. As unwelcome, drop-in company, emotional and physical pain try to usurp my home's peace and joy. Yet, when I'm most desperate for relief, Jesus ushers the pain far away. Few realize that I know pain so well.

On television, I appear as a confident Christian author, speaker, singer, and founder of Bright Light Ministry. But, within the doors of my heart and home, I'm a very sensitive little girl who leans heavily on Jesus' shoulders for strength.

Pain pushes buttons to make me feel weak. Yet, *without weakness, one never knows true strength.* How do I know? I'm overloaded with weaknesses and weakening situations, yet Jesus supplies abundant, enabling strength. And, when situations like caregiving drain strength, only Jesus replenishes the spirit.

Caregiving speeds the process of pearl making. I know this fact personally. Here is a snapshot of how I obtained a few of my pearls through caregiving and supporting caregivers in my family:

As a granddaughter of a caregiver, niece of a caregiver, cousin of caregivers, daughter of a caregiver, and caregiver myself, I've wrestled with the heavyweight champion called heartache. I have desperately desired cures for my precious, sick loved ones. I've lingered long on my heavenly Father's lap and, like a baby reaching for her daddy, I've stretched out my hand to touch His face and feel His presence. I've reached for His face many times. Yes, I'm very sensitive to others' pain.

My extreme sensitivity is a card with two sides: One side says, "Selfish." The other side says, "Caregiver." Over time and through rough lessons, I've learned how to flip my sensitivity to the "Caregiver" side.

Other than evangelism, caregiving is the ultimate calling for Christians. Christians need to love others actively by giving care to the physically hurting, emotionally pained, and spiritually sick. (I believe that full-time caregivers to physically ill people are beautiful and precious to the Lord.) Sometimes, giving care connotes caregiving for a physically ill loved one. In my tiny family, this has happened often.

According to fast-food sizes, my family would be classified as extra small, but our love would be called super-super-super-sized. (I have my parents, Aunt Ruth, Grandma Hilda, and a sister. That's all. No first cousins. No uncles.)

Perhaps my close, small family made me bond with my grandparents and adopted relatives even more. I know the gorgeous, glorious gleam of unconditional love. But I also know that strong bonds, when pulled apart by death and disease, shoot sharp, strong pain through the spines of our souls.

Papa Ray had Alzheimer's and died; Grandma Hilda has arteriosclerosis; Daddy has severe health problems and was once in a coma; Grandma Alice had congestive heart failure and recently died; Papa Otto suffered through severe pain and arthritis and died; my adopted uncle died of cancer; friends have cancer; and I have some chronic health problems. In each situation aforementioned, I have either supported the caregiver or been the caregiver. Oh, the pearls thereof . . .

Yet I have exciting news: Jesus gave me a ministry that caters to the needs that I once had. Through Bright Light Ministry, I actually pray with hurting people, counsel, volunteer, teach workshops, present dramas, and sing to alleviate pain and educate people to become pain relievers. Romans 8:28–30 and 2 Corinthians 1:3–5 are real to me. I realize firsthand that caregiving is painful. Here's a fictional entry that represents the pain of 56 million current caregivers in the United States:

> *Dear Journal,*
> *I haven't written in months. I've just been too busy caring for John . . . Today, I cleaned up the house—some. I couldn't do it all because John needed to be cleaned up—again.*
> *Now, I perform the job of full-time nurse 24/7. I'm worn out. But I'm really scared that I'm going to forget to give John his medicine at the right time. Today, I also felt like an unappreciated chauffeur because I shuttled John to and from doctors. John was testy and downright mean. (It's all part of his affliction, but it's still hard to take.)*
> *I wonder—Could I hire a caregiver for a caregiver? I need one.*
> —Caregiver

STACIE RUTH STOELTING knows pain, but she also knows Jesus' great joy! At fifteen, she wrote her acclaimed first book, *Still Holding Hands*, depicting her grandparents' romance and victory over Alzheimer's. At seventeen, she started Bright Light Ministry to beam Jesus' bright light to families in crisis. At twenty, she sang for President Bush. Grammy winners and her sister, Carrie, joined her to worship the heavenly King on *Heavenly!*, her upcoming CD. Visit www.brightlightministry.com.

There were times when I felt like writing the previous journal entry. But I learned two things about pain-induced growth via caregiving:

1. *Jesus is the Caregiver for the caregiver.* He sends care directly and indirectly through people, services, and aids.

2. *When life gets hard, let Jesus be your Security Guard.* He will guard your heart.

3. *When our souls' wells run dry, Jesus grants free refills.* Let Him fill you with His living water.

Yes, through pain, my Lord holds me tighter, my faith makes me a fighter, and my luminescent pearls gleam brighter. Now, I share my pearl necklace to encourage others.

Lisa, you are to God precious Romans 8:37-39

Sarah M

THERE IS HOPE

*Jeremiah 29:11 (NIV): "For I know the plans
I have for you," declares the Lord, "plans to prosper you and
not to harm you, plans to give you a hope and a future."*

Hope Lives

 The doctor was still speaking, but I didn't hear his words anymore. His voice sounded far away, like I was listening from underwater. I couldn't focus on him. Inside, I was screaming, *No, no, no!*

Until then, everything had been going well. I'd passed the critical first three months of pregnancy. We planned the best nursery a baby had ever seen—bright colors, cute pictures, comfy bed. After six years of marriage, we were excited to welcome our first child.

I felt tired that Sunday afternoon, but that wasn't unusual. Exhaustion was my first symptom of pregnancy. When I got up from a nap, there was a red stain on my grandmother's hand-stitched quilt. I phoned my doctor's emergency service and waited.

When the doctor called, he was encouraging at first, and I felt relieved. Just rest, stay off my feet, phone back if symptoms got worse. But, I wondered if the answering service's message had clearly communicated that stain's size and depth, soaking through to the blanket. After I explained, he said, "You need to go to the emergency room now. I'll meet you there."

What he determined that afternoon shocked me. Our child's life was gone. I'd never considered that possibility, even while I was driving to meet the doctor. I wanted a happy family. That was always one of my greatest desires. My husband and I were happy, but my vision of life included children. I'd do whatever I could for a child, but I was powerless to fix this. I couldn't control my future by exerting my will. I wasn't the master of this fate.

I finally pulled myself back into the present in that cheerless hospital room, asking my desperate questions. Why? What had I done to cause this? What could I have done to prevent it? What would the future be? Even with modern medicine, the doctor didn't really have answers to my questions. He didn't know why, or how, or if it would happen again, but he said nothing I'd done had caused it.

He called it a "missed abortion," an incomplete miscarriage. My child of promise, no longer living and growing, was still held fast by the womb prepared to nourish him. It would take time for that womb to relax, letting go. Then the doctor would remove it with less risk of damage to me. Without that procedure done and done well, I could never hope for another child.

The waiting period between the emergency room visit and the outpatient D & C was a heart-wrenching time, my hope and dream lying lifeless inside me. I stayed home from work. I couldn't face concerned questions about how I was doing. I couldn't say I was fine. I wasn't, but I couldn't express my intense grief, either. The longing. The fear. The doubt. My wounds of heart were hidden, but real, nonetheless.

I mourned an unborn child whose face I hadn't seen, whose hand I hadn't held. The depth of my feeling surprised me. In high school, I remember debating the topic of when life began, at conception or birth. Being a skilled debater, I could make a winning argument for either side. But now I knew an absolute truth. Just as the child John in Elizabeth's womb recognized Jesus in Mary's womb, I recognized the presence of my child. I'd never be the same.

Even in anguished moments, though, I felt God's comfort around me, through my husband and others. They cared with kind, simple words, hugs, calls, and notes. They allowed me time to mourn in my own way, a process that varies with each person, each loss. I did what Elisabeth Elliot did as she grieved for her husband, Jim. I found strength to do the one next thing I needed to do, then the next, and so on. For me that next thing was going back to work.

In time, the sharp pain of grief subsided. Step-by-step, I smiled and laughed again. I enjoyed daily life. Without knowing what my future held, I trusted my dreams would be restored, or God would give me new dreams. I celebrated life and love, encouraging everyone to do the same. I comforted others with the comfort I received.

Someday, I will see my child's face. I will hold his hand. He's dancing now through heaven's golden streets in the continual light of God's presence. He's joyously anticipating the day he'll greet me face-to-face. For though his time on earth was brief, our bond lasts throughout eternity.

SARAH CHAPMAN MCMANUS (www.Sarah ChapmanMcManus.com) writes and speaks to encourage people to live life to the max. A few of her favorite things are food, friends, family, fun, faith, and the fantasy of finishing her to-do list some-day. She and husband, David, live in Illinois. They enjoy traveling and visiting their grown children in Tennessee.

OUR ETERNAL FATHER WANTS
WHAT IS BEST FOR US

Romans 8:15 (from Word on the Street, paraphrase by
Rob Lacey, Zondervan, 2004): What you were given
was the certificate of being a daughter, for by his Spirit
we get to call the totally awesome God, "Dad"!

Finding My Father

My dad was short for a man, but what he lacked in stature he made up for in character. Gracious and generous, full of integrity, wit, and charm, he was a committed, caring doctor whose patients respected him, and a warm and wonderful father who believed his girls could achieve anything. Even when I decided to follow Christ—a shock for a Jewish dad—then subsequently "married out" to a man who became a Christian minister, he never let it diminish his love for me. In fact, when I told him that he would have his name in the official Guinness family tree and pedigree, as my husband-to-be was a great, great grandson of the famous Irish brewer, he quipped straight back, "And did you have to pick a poor relative?"

The nightmare began when, in his late fifties, this dignified and lovely man began to disappear behind a mask, as a series of minor brain haemorrhages drove him into a world where I could no longer reach him. At first, I thought that if I prayed and fought hard enough, I could somehow bring him back. But I was no match for dementia. He who had always protected me, said he'd always be there for me, abandoned me, not in a moment, but little by little. Not as he used to pull the sticking plasters from my cuts and grazes in one tear-jerking, hair-removing sweep, as doctors do, but bit by bit, pulling and dragging and prolonging the agony.

I wondered whether he knew how we nursed and cared for him, as he had nursed and cared for so many. I hope he didn't. I hope the disease was merciful to him, even if it wasn't to us. I railed against God. How could He allow the sad, slow destruction of so many fine faculties?

My tears went on year after year for almost six years, until, when the final moment came, I was left feeling empty, desolate, defenceless, and fatherless. I would want for nothing as long as he was there, my dad had said, but he wasn't there anymore, and I badly wanted his pride in me and in the grandchildren he would never know. I never had time to show him how I would use all the riches he passed on to me.

"People must always come before principles, for without love people of principle become fanatics."

"Do to others as you would have them do to you."

"Always examine both sides of every story."

And then, after Dad died, a strange thing happened. I don't know what his relationship with God was at the end, but my husband, Peter, had read to him from the Scriptures, and he appeared to respond. I prayed so hard that God would show me he was safe, and as I did so, dozens of beautiful, long-forgotten memories flooded back in full Technicolour—Dad singing by my bed and playing his ukulele, jangling the coins in his pocket as we stopped at the confectionary shop on the way home from school, buying the teachers cream cakes on school sports' days, playing cricket with us in the street, dancing the twist when it was the latest rage, savouring good red wine, admiring a fine pair of female legs. What a man he was! And how I laughed. It felt as if he had been given back to me.

I keep on finding him now—in my attitudes and goals, and in the dreams he dreamed for me, so many of which, though he could not see it, have been fulfilled in Jesus, the Messiah. Most of all, I recognise his influence in the way I see God. Because of my earthly father, I have found a generous, joyous heavenly Dad whose love is rock solid, who takes me in His arms when I'm hurting, who believes in me, thinks I'm beautiful, cheers me on, and denies me nothing unless it's best for me. This Dad will never change or decay. He will never abandon me. I shall never want again. Can any daughter wish for more?

MICHELE GUINNESS was born into a Jewish family and is now married to an Anglican clergyman. She is a public relations and communications consultant, and also works as a freelance journalist and writer. She has written several bestselling books, including *Child of the Covenant* and *A Little Kosher Seasoning*.

KEEP GOD FRONT AND CENTER
AND YOU'LL FIND THE TIME
TO ACCOMPLISH WHAT YOU NEED

Ecclesiastes 3:1, 5, 6 (NIV): There is a time for everything,
and a season for every activity under heaven. . . .
a time to scatter stones and a time to gather them . . .
a time to keep and a time to throw away.

Time

 Since I'm a stay-at-home mom, I have all day to clean and cook and take care of small home repairs, pay bills, do laundry, and create decorative centerpieces out of pipe cleaners, pinecones, and spray paint.

So why is it when 10:00 p.m. arrives, I look around at the house, the dishes piled in the sink, the stack of paperwork awaiting my attention, the cereal spilled on the floor, and the still unfolded clothes, and I think to myself, "What did I do all day?" I've seriously considered the possibility that there's something interrupting the time-space continuum in my house; a force field of sorts. Most days I go, go, go to the point of forgetting to take a minute to stop and eat. So, why is everything in disarray come bedtime? Where did my time go?

I often wish there were just a couple more hours in the day. I'm always saying that I don't have enough time to do all I have to do. Too often I feel as if I'm drowning in a sea of chores that I will never, ever be able to accomplish. And I know I'm not alone. In fact, during worship service last month, we had a drama about this very thing. My friends are always talking about this very subject. We feel like failures when we can't do everything, and do it in a timely and very precise manner. We have so much pressure to be perfect that we get depressed when we fall short. And as humans, we always fall short.

The other day when I felt like I was drowning, my friend Michelle forwarded me an e-mail with a devotional on this very subject. Reading the devotional, I began to have a new outlook on time. Time is a gift and we all have the same number of hours in a day. It's just a question of how we're using that gift of time. At the end of the day, we don't want to be like the man in Isaiah 49:4 who said, "I have used up my strength but have accomplished nothing."

If we don't seem to have enough time, perhaps we're filling our days with tasks that really aren't important. Oftentimes I find myself doing something that isn't necessarily bad, but it's probably not the best choice for my time. I'm notorious for getting distracted playing solitaire on my computer. That's not a *bad* thing to do, but it isn't a wise choice when I have laundry to be folded, bills to be paid, or kids running around the house like maniacs because they're bored and want to play with me.

I once saw a demonstration on time and priorities. Take a jar and fill it with sand. The sand represents all the things we have to do, actually all the "little" things in our lives. Next, put a large rock into the jar—the rock stands for God. But if the jar—your life—is already filled with sand, there's no room for God. So . . . empty the jar and try again. Now put the rock in first; put God first in all things, including your time. *Now,* fill the rest of the jar with sand. What happens? There's plenty of room for God, who is the Rock, *and* for all the other things that take up your time.

So concentrate on the things that have to be done first. Yeah, yeah, this is much easier said than done. Sometimes it's difficult to log off the computer and write out the bills. Sometimes we just want to sit down for a minute and watch TV even though we know we should be planning dinner or running errands or vacuuming the house. And of course, little kids at home can foul up your best-laid plans. You plan on cleaning the bathroom, but instead, thanks to your little ones, you end up scrubbing pudding off the ceiling, or cleaning dirty footprints off the kitchen counter, or giving impromptu baths because the kids thought it would be a good idea to decorate their hair with maple syrup and baby powder. Not that any of these things have ever happened to me . . .

Anyway, it's always a good idea to stop, take a deep breath, and think about how you're spending your time. I believe God gives us enough time to accomplish what He wants us to do. If you aren't finishing all your tasks, ask yourself, "Is this really what I should be doing right now?" Maybe it's time to eliminate some of those time robbers. And remember to put first things first. Keep your eye on God and everything else will fall into place. And remember that it's okay to say no to those extras you just don't have time for right now. Unless, of course, it's your kids calling to you from the other side of the house, saying, "Moooom, can you come here a minute? I think the toilet's exploding!" In that case, I suggest you stop the important things you're doing and go. Very fast.

DAWN MEEHAN writes a popular blog on which she makes light of her life as a stay-at-home mom of six children. She's also the author of the humorous parenting book *Because I Said So*. Dawn lives in the Chicago area with her family and stays busy changing diapers, cleaning pudding off her ceiling, tackling insurmountable piles of laundry, and pulling her kids out of trees. www.becauseisaidso.com/.

GIVE YOUR GUTS TO GOD FIRST

*Isaiah 58:10–11 (NASB): And if you give yourself to the hungry
and satisfy the desire of the afflicted, then your light will rise
in the darkness and your gloom will become like midday. And the Lord
will continually guide you and satisfy your desire in scorched places,
and give strength to your bones; and you will be like a watered garden,
And like a spring of water whose waters do not fail.*

Spill Your Guts to God First

 In high school, right after I met Jesus, I was so desperate for healing from traumatic childhood issues that I stopped every Christian I knew and spilled my guts to them.

I craved empathy. I needed help. Eventually, by God's grace, He healed me during my college years when countless folks were praying for me. By my twenties, I no longer felt the need to share my painful childhood.

Eventually, though, I sensed a need for deeper healing, and began to share again. I was cautious about it, and often very strategic about which friends I would trust with that information.

Through some recent injury, though, I've fallen back into the over-disclosure I exhibited as a teenager. I've realized afresh that I am sharing, not to benefit my hearer, but to garner empathy for myself. Eventually I came to see that I was replacing my deep need for God's healing with mere human empathy.

And I was doing this as I spoke in front of audiences.

I'm thankful for two discerning friends who kindly, but firmly, pointed this out to me. They critiqued a message I'd given to a crowd of women in Munich, Germany. Hearing my message from an audience's perspective was excruciating. Much of what I shared dealt with my own personal struggle and very little about what could help those dear women. I spewed my pain, highlighted all the wrongs committed against me, and walked my audience down a painful road in my life, all without offering hope or practical help.

After realizing I was saying all these things, I knew I wanted to change. I didn't want my speaking presentations to be the Mary-DeMuth-Need-for-Empathy Show. I desired to be the kind of speaker who delivered life-giving messages of hope, words that deeply benefited my audiences. I no longer wanted to spill my own angst and need upon them.

What does that mean for me in a practical way today?

I need to take my injuries-du-jour and place them squarely at the feet of the One who experienced every human pain. The One who understands. The High Priest who sympathizes with all my weaknesses. The Healer. The God of all comfort.

That's where my vulnerability needs to go first. To spill my guts to God. To gain His empathy. To be healed by Him initially. My primary focus must be giving my hurts to Jesus through prayer, eventually becoming someone who helps others with their wounds. That's not to say I won't be vulnerable in front of my audiences, but that I've been willing to give my traumas and trials to Jesus first, daring to walk with Him through the healing. In doing this, I'm actually blessing those who listen to me instead of using them as empathy bearers. And my focus shifts from getting my needs filled to filling others.

Isaiah 58:10–11 highlights the beauty of what God will do when we run to Him and seek to fill others:

And if you give yourself to the hungry
And satisfy the desire of the afflicted,
Then your light will rise in the darkness
And your gloom will become like midday.
And the Lord will continually guide you
And satisfy your desire in scorched places,

And give strength to your bones;
And you will be like a watered garden,
And like a spring of water whose waters do not fail.

What a blessing those verses are! I need to retool the way I speak, so my focus is on giving myself to the hungry and satisfying the desire of the afflicted (instead of always revealing my own hunger, and seeking to satisfy my own desire through them). And I need to let Jesus make me a watered garden, to let Him satiate me in my scorched places, to let Him be the wellspring of life inside. Because, really, I can't give what I don't have.

. . . .

MARY E. DEMUTH is a novelist, speaker and book mentor who loves to help people turn their trials into triumph. Author of three parenting books and three novels, her latest novel is *Daisy Chain*. She has three children, two pets, and one husband. They all live in harmony in the great state of Texas. Find Mary at www.marydemuth.com or www.thewritingspa.com.

Oh, how I need Jesus to free me from myself! To fill me up to the brim so I can fill others by His strength.

I still struggle sharing my pain with others in order to gain the empathy I should be seeking in Jesus. My mouth trips me up. Even so, I don't want to be the wounded person who can't stop telling her story of injury. I don't want to make human empathy my sole goal in life. Not when Jesus stands near, offering me the best empathy I can fathom, He who takes my spilled guts and makes something beautiful. For His sake. And mine. And others, too.

EMBRACE YOUR LIFE

*James 1:2–4 (CEV): My friends, be glad, even if you have a lot
of trouble. You know that you learn to endure by having your faith tested.
But you must learn to endure everything, so that you will be
completely mature and not lacking in anything.*

Perfect Delusions

 As a child, I always longed for the "perfect" life. Naturally, I wasn't too sure what that entailed, but I knew it would be vastly different from my own life of divorced parents, working mom, TV dinners, and too much independence. In my mind, the perfect life would be like those old TV reruns I loved to watch—family shows like *Donna Reed, Leave It to Beaver,* and *Ozzie and Harriet.* Someday I wanted to be like them—mom and dad and kids and the picket fence too!

When I was in my early twenties, I married a great guy, and just weeks before our first anniversary, we had our first son. Sixteen months later, we had our second. Okay, it was a little overwhelming, but with two adorable little boys, I felt we were well on our way to becoming a perfect imitation of Ozzie and Harriet Nelson—eighties style. We even had the Cape Cod house and station wagon to prove it.

Okay, everything wasn't totally perfect, but not for a lack of trying. Unlike the way I'd grown up, I was determined to do things *right* for my family. I cooked real dinners and served them with style. I cleaned house like an overly caffeinated Merry Maid. I gardened and sewed and served as president of the PTA. I taught women's Bible studies and even brought in some extra cash with part-time jobs. I was a regular little Proverbs 31 woman. And for the most part, life was going smoothly—almost perfectly. Or so I thought.

Until my sons entered their teen years and my "perfect" little world began to fall apart.

Like a devastating tsunami, teen rebellion, alcohol, drugs, and even mental illness slammed into ideal life. Try as I might, I discovered that I couldn't control things anymore. My "perfect" home and family and hopes were being crushed and swept away right before my eyes.

By high school, my younger son had rebelled against every value we'd attempted to teach him. He wanted to dress like Marilyn Manson, refused to attend church, and focused his artistic abilities on creating hellish-looking images. Plus, he belonged to a garage rock band that played disturbingly dark music. It wasn't long before he began experimenting with alcohol and marijuana. We did what we could and hoped he was just going through a phase. But not long after graduating high school, he got hooked on methamphetamines. And we were devastated.

If that were not bad enough, our older son, at age twenty was diagnosed and treated for schizophrenia. This seemed like the final blow. I felt as if, not only had our family been wiped out by the terrible tsunami, I now resided in the belly of the whale. For a short time it seemed that darkness, hopelessness, despair were my only companions.

But God was there too. And, like a lifeline, He was holding my hand.

I clung to God's hand like I'd never clung before. I knew that without Him, I would drown. In fact, sure there were days when I almost wanted to drown—simply to escape the pain. But I knew that, as much as I needed God, my sons needed me to be strong. And I can honestly say that God's strength was compensating for my weakness. Because it's only when we come to the end of ourselves that God is able to step in and take over.

Now, although God was strengthening me, I still had to make my way through the mess that my life had become. My husband and I had to join forces and figure out how to best help our sons through their crises. We began to learn firsthand why Jesus told us to live one day at a time. A single day usually had more than enough to overwhelm us. And I can't begin to count the number of times I cried out to God in the middle of the night, begging Him to save, protect, and deliver our sons. Even when things got better, I still felt shaky . . . or perhaps just shaken.

And what about my childhood desire for that ideal life? What about imitating Ozzie and Harriet? Ironically, we'd done a pretty good job of mirroring their *real* lives. They too had managed to look good on the exterior, but there were problems beneath. One of their sons (also a musician) had a serious drug problem. Go figure.

Now, as a writer for the Christian market, I felt challenged on two levels. First of all, what would other Christians think if they knew what was really going on in our Christian home? Second, how could I continue to write without being honest and transparent about all areas of my life?

And so, like it says in James 1:2–4, I chose to welcome trials. I decided to embrace my messy life and to let go of my warped ideals of perfection. My life would be an open book for anyone who wanted to look in. I wouldn't hide anything. If that meant my writing career was over, so be it.

Come to find out, God wasn't ready to end my writing career. Not only that, but it seemed as if the trials and challenges I'd gone through actually improved my writing. Soon I was writing for teens—telling stories about imperfections and heartaches. And a few years down the road, I was even able to write novels about schizophrenia and drug addiction.

By choosing to embrace my life—to welcome the ongoing trials as friends—I continue to learn that only God can perfect me. But it's not in that twisted outward way that I had once perceived as perfection. His is a quiet transformation that changes me inwardly, and in a way where He's the one to receive the glory. And that is the only way to live a truly perfect life.

MELODY CARLSON is the author of more than a hundred books for women, teens, and children. She lives with her husband in Oregon where they enjoy camping, biking, and hiking in the beautiful Northwest. Recent book releases include *Limelight, 86 Bloomberg Place,* and *The Carter House Girls.*

TACKLE THE TOUGH QUESTIONS

1 Thessalonians 5:17 (KJV): Pray without ceasing.

Thy Will Be Done?

Many years ago my sister, Margaret, twenty-two years of age at the time, was killed in an automobile accident. She had just graduated from Florida State University and was serving as a summer missionary to Native Americans in Oklahoma before attending seminary that fall to prepare herself to go as a missionary to China. Her life ended abruptly one week before her home mission work was completed.

At my parents' request, these words were carved on her tombstone: "Thy will be done." Somehow they helped assuage my parents' grief, but these words stirred up angry feelings in me. I asked God, "Is this the way You reward someone who loves You and serves You? Did You really care about Margaret's life? How can I ever pray 'Thy will be done' in my life too and mean it?"

I had to make peace with the will of God. Somehow I couldn't see the forest for the trees. On a personal basis, I can now welcome God's will into my own life for I believe that He wants me to grow toward spiritual maturity in Jesus Christ. He wants me to grow toward becoming my finest self, and I can grow only in the power of a personal faith relationship with Jesus. And as I grow, God wants me to reach out and bring others to Him that they too might grow in Christ. You know within this larger context of the will of God, no human circumstance or tragic event is ever beyond the redemptive power of God. As I expectantly abide in God's ongoing will, He can work creatively for good in every situation and help me keep on growing as I reach up to Him and out to others.

At the time of my sister's death, someone gave me a copy of Leslie Weatherhead's book *The Will of God.* He presents three aspects of the will of God. First, the intentional will of God—that is His ideal plan for mankind. Second, the circumstantial will of God—God's plan within certain circumstances. And third, the ultimate will of God—His final realization of His purposes.

God's intentional or ideal will for Margaret, that she serve Him by serving as a missionary while she herself continued to grow in Christ, had been thwarted by the human circumstances of the driver's losing control of the car in which she was riding. Even then God could have miraculously spared her life, but being a Christian missionary did not automatically exempt Margaret from God's physical laws. Mercifully God took her home within the context of His circumstantial will. God's intentional, or ideal will, had been thwarted, but His circumstantial will, I believe, was accomplished.

God's ultimate will, His final realization of His purposes in Margaret's life that she be a blessing and influence many lives for Christ, triumphed even in her untimely death, for her life continues to bear fruit today. Honorary pallbearers at her funeral service were members of the Margaret Turnage Life Service Band named in her honor. While earning her way through college as secretary in a local Baptist church, she had organized a group of some thirty-six young people and college students who met regularly to pursue God's will in their vocation. As my sister's college roommate, I had heard her pray often by name for each one of them. From that group have come many dedicated Christian leaders scattered around the world, all profoundly influenced by her life. And needless to say, her life left rich deposits in my life, too.

I learned the sequel to the story only recently. The driver who had lost control of the car in which my sister was killed was a young Native

American. He was deeply affected by Margaret's life and her death. As a result, he opened up his own life to the will of God. For many years now he has been faithful in serving as a Baptist pastor to Native Americans in Oklahoma.

. . . .

CAROLYN RHEA passed away in 2003. This essay was transcribed from a speech she gave at a church in 1979. Prior to her death, she established the Margaret Turnage Student Missionary Scholarship Fund at Palm Beach Atlantic University. God's ultimate will for Margaret continues as a new generation participates in missionary trips.

The spiritual quality of Margaret's personhood in Jesus Christ was a dynamic force that God used creatively for good in the lives of many people. As Margaret grew toward spiritual maturity in Jesus Christ, she reached out and brought others to Christ that they too might grow in Him.

Touching the near edges of her immediate world for Jesus Christ was her priority. And in so doing, she continues to touch the far edges, too.

To Lisa –
many Blessings,
Maureen Lang

MAUREEN LANG

LEARNING FROM THE TRIALS OF OUR PARENTS HELPS MAKE US STRONG

James 1:2–4 (NASB): Consider it all joy, my brethren, when you encounter various trials, knowing that the testing of your faith produces endurance. And let endurance have its perfect result, so that you may be perfect and complete, lacking in nothing.

Proof of Strength . . . It's in the Genes

"She lived an interesting life."

That's what people said a number of years ago when my grandmother died. She survived the loss of her mother and sister when she herself was just six years old and consequently sent to an orphanage when her father was told he couldn't raise her alone. She lived through two world wars, the Great Depression, an unhappy marriage, and the loss of her only daughter from pneumonia at seven years old. A few years later she withstood a divorce during a time in society when it was newsy enough to be printed in the local paper.

Interesting? Perhaps. But when I look at those things that would be labeled "interesting," they're undeniably tied to those things that made my grandmother strong.

Perhaps since my father had seen his mother face her challenges, he was strengthened for the obstacles he would face: being the child of a divorce, seeing his father woo another woman and her son with expensive gifts he'd never seen, not even on birthdays or Christmas. And later, did he remember his mother's grit when he was captured by the Japanese and held as a POW for three and a half years?

So when my own challenges came (as challenges inevitably do in life), when the initial pain subsided enough to ponder, to gather strength, it should have been easy to remind myself of a few things. I wasn't the first, and certainly wouldn't be the last in my family to face sorrow. I came from good, strong, *survivors* stock.

My son was just over a year old when we were told he would be limited by mental retardation. My husband and I learned to set aside the hopeful expectations we had held for our son's "normal" life. But as the years went by, we learned to set aside even those adjusted expectations accompanying the diagnosis of Fragile X Syndrome. Our son's disability proved to be profound rather than mild or moderate, and he will always need assistance to get through a day.

So now when I tire of changing diapers, when I find myself frustrated over pages torn from books, yet another broken lamp, the messes left in the kitchen from a boy who's been developmentally two years old for over a dozen years now, I remind myself the task to raise this little boy wasn't bestowed upon just anyone. I was groomed for it in the stories from my grandmother, in the memories my father told of his captivity, in the knowledge that with God there are no accidents, not even genetically. And those challenges set a life apart from "normal" to "interesting."

What were you groomed for? What strength did you see proven in those who went before you in your family? Or maybe you can learn from the mistakes made in your family tree. Usually it's a combination of strengths and weaknesses we learn from the most.

Every life has a story behind it. Whether yours is "interesting" or not, the disappointments you face, the frustrations to your goals, the mistakes that need to be rectified, all lead to the realization and proof of strength we didn't know we had. Those steps can also lead upward, toward God, who tells us time and time again in the Bible that testing produces endurance, and that the suffering we bear here will be rewarded in heaven.

MAUREEN LANG is an award-winning author of eight novels. She resides in the Midwest with her husband, two boys, and Susie, their dog. Visit her website at www.maureenlang.com.

OUR VALUE RESTS IN GOD

Zephaniah 3:17 (NIV): The Lord your God is with you,
he is mighty to save. He will take great delight in you, he will
quiet you with his love, he will rejoice over you with singing.

No End in Sight

 Months ago, when the phone rang at 4:00 a.m., I learned that Jennie, my former sister-in-law, is in the ICU. How?

Just last weekend, she ran the minimarathon. In the final stretch, her sons ran beside her, their hands in hers. She just wanted one picture of them all crossing the finish line together, but I had forgotten my camera and she was peeved at me.

As I started my two-hour drive to the hospital, my thoughts scan my twenty-year relationship with Jennie. Jennie and I married brothers. We share the same first and last name, but we are very different, and we spent fifteen years trying to outdo each other. She became the perfect stay-at-home mom, and now was in pharmaceutical sales; her divorce drove her to work. I, the driven physician, recently quit work to stay home.

Ten years ago, pregnant within a week of Jennie with our firsts, I miscarried. Together by chance in the waiting room, sharing the same doctor, the nurse calls our name and I jump up, only to hear the nurse say, "Not you, honey, I need the pregnant one." The searing pain of that loss, then, yet knowing now God's plan, and to think my daughter would not be, if that miscarriage had not happened to me.

When I first met Jennie, I liked her despite our differences. She enjoyed pageants; I preferred waterskiing. In her old album, our first picture: I am hugging her in my frumpy T-shirt and shorts, she dressed in her ball gown and crown. The friction started to sizzle between us shortly after that. I remember being "the fiancée" at the Olympics with my future in-laws; she, just "the girlfriend," yet there were memory bricks in the Olympic village ordered for everyone, Jennie included, except me. A simple oversight, but a rivalry started for me. I nursed my insecurities over my career choice, my commitment to my family, my appearance. I had a vivid picture of myself at the family events in leftover lumpy clothes, Jennie tucked into crisp linen, matching hat, French-tipped toes. We barely spoke. Her presence in my life felt abrasive, uncomfortable, like grit. The shatter of her divorce changed us.

We covet: wanting to be the pretty one, the smart one, the athlete, the doctor, the married one, the first or best mother. Through Jennie's painful divorce, God took my self-made competition, stripped me down, and melted the hardness of my heart toward Jennie. God made me face and name the darkness in my heart, jealous pride, and then He said, "Let it go." Wednesday church suppers, Sunday worship, we did these together after her divorce. By the grace of God, I became her family after she technically left mine, and my rival became my friend.

Arriving, finally, I park the car. The hospital is a dead zone, quiet, artificial. Outside the ICU, the story spills. Jennie and her date were celebrating her successful race. He left to use the restroom. She took a bite of her steak, choked, quietly rose, and tried to make it to the bathroom. A server asked her if she was choking. She nodded. She collapsed during the Heimlich maneuver, no pulse, no life.

Lingering in a seven-day coma, Jennie never woke up. She died one day before Mother's Day. Scanning hours of TV footage, I glimpsed half a second of Jennie, her arms down, bobbing toward the finish line, the boys lost from view. At thirty-four, Jennie left us, running strong, no end in sight.

Her death hit me like a punch in the stomach. I spent weeks looking through twenty years, grasping for any picture of her living, breathing body, the back of her leg, her hand, her feet. A photograph in my wedding album shows Jennie putting on makeup, her eyes staring at you in the mirror; dried peonies rest on the hat brim and frame her face. Going through her things, I found that bridesmaid's hat in a box on top of her Derby hats, kept and precious to her. Jennie moved several times after my wedding. She had lots of opportunities to throw it away.

Jennie loved me. When I stopped defining myself in my comparisons to Jennie, and became her friend, God showed me that my value rests in Him. He delights in me, sings over me, and quiets my jealous heart. God transformed the grit of my envy of Jennie into the pearl of my affection for her. She knew I genuinely loved her, before she died, and I am so grateful for that.

As the daughter of an Air Force helicopter pilot, Jenny moved more than thirty times during her childhood. She retired from her career in medicine in 2007 to spend more time with her husband and her children. Her family lives in Danville, Kentucky. Jenny spends her free time competing in triathlons and marathons. The first annual Jennie Carol Memorial Mother's Day 5k took place in Danville this past May. All the proceeds went to Backpack Kids, a national program that sends backpacks of food to serve children in need over the weekends. She can be contacted at jgtarter@kywimax.com.

SEEK HIS COMFORT AND GUIDANCE
WHEN YOU EXPERIENCE FEAR

Isaiah 41:10 (NIV): So do not fear, for I am with you;
do not be dismayed for I am your God.
I will strengthen you and help you; I will uphold you
with my righteous right hand.

Bigger than Fear

 Even though I wasn't a Christian at the time, I believed marriage was sacred . . . even an abusive one.

I was hanging in there for the sake of my daughter. That's what I told myself. My husband was unfaithful, unpredictable, unapologetic, and downright scary. I never knew what might set him off, and after the first few smacks across my face, I cowered inside if he just gave me one of *those* looks. The anticipation of violence became more frightening than the actual blows. But he was always repentant once he calmed down. He wanted to be a better person. He promised to get counseling.

How could I say no? We had a daughter together. She deserved a complete family. So I kept trying, for her.

Then I heard about her uncontrollable shaking when I wasn't around. God blessed me with discernment. What was I teaching my daughter by attempting to endure domestic violence? I didn't need to stay for her; I needed to *leave* for her. The next time my husband beat me, God blessed me with the strength to gather up my child and get away.

He also blessed me with strength. I didn't even know He was around, yet He blessed me.

My husband actually cried while he begged me to try again. It was hard to say no. But the first time he came to visit our girl, she looked at his expression and grabbed on to me. That three-year-old child told her daddy, "Don't hit Mommy." Only God could make me go back to the man who had put such fear in my child and me. But God didn't make me go back. He blessed me for standing firm and breaking the cycle into which my husband and I had fallen.

He blessed me with assurance. He blessed me with guidance. I was still clueless about His being around. Yet He was taking care of me.

As a single mom I struggled. At times I felt helpless, especially those times when a man would have been handy around the apartment. The financial situation was tight. I had to save up just to take my girl to a movie. But my daughter, now a lovely young woman, doesn't remember our being poor. She remembers the fun she and I had together whenever I was home from work. We still laugh about the time we made our own popcorn for the movies and stuffed a warm gallon-sized baggie down her sweater, hoping no one at the theater would question the oddly shaped little girl who smelled strangely of butter. She remembers the Very Merry Unbirthdays we celebrated together whenever we felt like it, finding silly trinkets around the house to give each other after blowing out our candles on the lopsided cake we had made together. She remembers our trips to museums and the pumpkin patch and the library. She remembers laughing together about so many things—we hadn't laughed much during the marriage.

And she remembers when I found Christ. For me, everything changed. But my daughter took a little longer to find Him. We had a few rough years while her heart wandered far enough away to frighten me. Again, I felt helpless, and this time it would have been handy to have a *pastor* around the house. Yet Christ drew her to Him and swiftly drew my daughter back to me.

He blessed me with reconciliation. He blessed me with the salvation of my girl's soul. This time I knew exactly where the blessings were coming from.

The first time I heard my grown daughter counsel a friend whose husband was repeatedly violent, my heart melted. Her friend feared—just as I had—that her leaving would destroy her own little girl. My daughter said, "I know what you mean. But I'm thankful my mother got away when I was a kid. I learned from her that you can't let anyone do that to you, no matter how much you love him. And you and your daughter *will* survive if you go. Sometimes you survive *only* if you go. I learned that from my mother."

I had feared she would learn from me that marriage wasn't sacred. I had feared she would learn so much that wouldn't be good for her. But she learned—and I learned—that, because of God, because of His love, we need not fear at all.

The author of *Sunset Beach* (2009) and *Beach Dreams* (2008), **TRISH PERRY** discovered her love of writing while earning a degree in psychology. She switched career paths in 1997 and never looked back. Her debut novel, *The Guy I'm Not Dating*, placed second in the 2007 FHL Inspirational Readers' Choice Contest, and her second novel, *Too Good to Be True*, was a finalist in the 2008 FHL IRCC, the GRW Maggie Awards, and LCRW's Barclay Gold Awards. To learn more about Trish and her novels, visit www.trishperry.com.

WE ARE ALL CALLED TO BE
CHRIST IN THE WORLD

*Romans 8:9 (THE MESSAGE): If God himself
has taken up residence in your life,
you can hardly be thinking more
of yourself than of him.*

As Tough as Pearls

It was an unbearably hot day in New York City, the kind when the sun beats down on pavement clogged with cars and makes maneuvering down a crowded sidewalk feel like fighting one's way through a tropical jungle. I was no stranger to hand-to-hand combat those days, at war with much of my life: a broken engagement, difficulties at work, and the feeling that I, with my thirtieth birthday on the horizon, had no plan for my life.

On the way home, I ducked into the place that had become my habit to visit that summer: a small chapel off the grand St. Ignatius Loyola Church on Park Avenue. Early on weekday evenings, I attended a small service along with a handful of elderly well-dressed ladies who seemed genetically immune to the heat and humidity and the hustle and bustle of the city. They sat like little gray birds with colored wings in their pastels and summer whites. I slipped into the back pew, looking at them in awe noting the diamonds on their hands, the pearls at their throats. Week after week I watched them, wondering what their lives must be like, and surmising that they must be wives, mothers, and probably grandmothers.

Single and alone, with no family within several hundred miles, I held myself apart. As soon as the service was over, I left with barely a smile to the left or the right, feeling like a complete outsider. How must they see me? I wondered, and then decided I was probably invisible to ladies such as these, whose biggest concern was probably where to have lunch the next day. Or so I imagined.

Then he came in.

In the heat of an August day in New York City, the man gave off a gagging stench. As soon as he walked into the chapel, I buried my head in my folded hands and breathed through my mouth, all the while praying, "Please don't let him sit next to me. If he does, I'll have to leave."

Shaming thoughts rushed in on the heels of that prayer. Where was my compassion for this homeless man? He was my age, or so I'd guess, his large frame draped with several layers of jackets and coats despite the heat. No doubt he was mentally ill, and probably physically as well.

I challenged myself to see Christ in him, but I couldn't. I bowed my head again, this time in shame.

The man made his way slowly up the aisle of the chapel toward the front pew where the grandest lady of them all always took her seat. Over the weeks I had come to admire her style and classic features. In her youth, she must have been quite a beauty. When the man sat down, I saw her turn her head; the diamond earrings she wore sparkled in the sunlight angled through the window. "She'll get up now and leave," I thought to myself.

Instead, this lovely lady slid closer to the man and held out the prayer book to him, reading aloud every word and tracing each line with her finger. She never left his side the entire time, as gentle with him as any mother with her son. Sitting in the last pew of the small chapel, I watched her with a different kind of awe that day, not for her wardrobe or jewelry, but for the simple grace that she exuded.

No, I could not see Christ in the homeless man who shuffled

into the chapel that day. As hard as I tried, I could not get past the filthy rags and the offensive odor. But in the gentle expression of a Park Avenue matron, with all her diamonds and pearls, I found the compassionate face of my Lord and Savior.

PATRICIA CRISAFULLI spent fifteen years as a journalist, including as a correspondent for Reuters America. Eight years ago she became a "writer for hire," and since then has been a ghostwriter of more than a dozen books. She is also the author of the book *Remembering Mother, Finding Myself: A Journey of Love and Self-Acceptance* (written under the name Patricia Commins). Currently, she is at work on a novel. She lives in suburban Chicago with her husband and son.

GOD IS THE GREAT ORCHESTRATOR
OF THE UNEXPECTED

*2 Corinthians 4:17; 5:5, 7 (ESV): For this light momentary
affliction is preparing for us an eternal weight of glory
beyond all comparison . . . He who has prepared us for this
very thing is God . . . for we walk by faith, not by sight.*

"God Has Heard"

"Mom, I think my water broke!"

My younger daughter's voice on the phone was excited and tense. "And I'm never going back to that Olive Garden Restaurant again!" I burst out laughing at April's embarrassed response to her water breaking in a crowded restaurant, grabbed my purse, and hurried out to my car. As I drove to the hospital, I thought about all we had gone through with April over the past nine months.

Eighteen months earlier I had coached our older daughter, Megan, through the birth of her first baby. She and her husband were in a stable, Christian marriage, and the season of her pregnancy was one of joyous anticipation. My husband, Dennis, had a terminal illness, making expected grandbabies an especially poignant treasure.

April was pregnant, not married, and the father of our second grandchild was not a Christian, nor did he desire to parent his son. He had made appointments on two occasions for April to have an abortion and our heavy hearts were grateful that she had not acquiesced in that regard. Two daughters and two grandsons, two experiences with so much in common and such heart-wrenching differences.

At one point during the painful journey that was April's pregnancy, I sat curled up on the sofa, crying and praying. The thought pierced through me like a spear that there was nothing we could do to make this situation right. There was no good answer. When a first step is taken in disobedience to God, what follows will never be completely free from the tinge of sin and sorrow—a certain shadow remains.

But God, our blessed redeeming God, brings about unforeseen beauty and joy in spite of our sinful, stumbling steps. April agonized over the decision to keep her baby or give him up for adoption. We prayed and watched and ached for our daughter and grandson. Our friends' and extended family's opinions, advice, criticism, sympathy, anger, disappointment, and anxiousness whirled like a cyclone about us. After months of deliberation, April decided to give up her baby boy in open adoption.

The day she was given profiles of the prospective adoptive parents to review, she called me with unconfined excitement. "Mom, you won't believe this couple! They are incredible!" She described the couple who would eventually parent our grandson. They had a missionary background, were in full-time ministry, were musical, very active in their church, and loved dogs, just as we do. The husband had a master's degree, just as Dennis does, and their plan was for the wife to stay home and dedicate herself to caring for the baby they would adopt.

In the midst of the worst time of our lives, there was no denying that this couple and this baby were made-to-order for each other. The first name they chose for him means "God has heard," and they gave him the middle name that April had chosen.

I coached her through his birth and was not fully assured of what her final decision would be until she put the baby in his new parents' arms two days later. She whispered to him through her tears, "I am confident that I have made the right decision. I am doing this because I love you." I sobbed internally, inaudibly, the tears pouring down my face as I watched her give my grandson to another couple to raise. Birth mother and adoptive mother put their arms around each other with the baby between them as their tears mingled. We watched our daughter perform the most courageous, generous act of her life as our hearts crumbled in broken pieces at our feet and yet soared heavenward with gratitude. We watched the ecstatic new parents leave the hospital with their baby son, our grandson, the gift of a lifetime.

Following the most recent visit we had with the baby—as happy and healthy as could be—and his adoptive parents, I asked April, "Are you still confident of your decision?"

"More than ever, Mom. More than ever."

NANETTE SWICK was born to missionary parents in Jamaica and grew up in the Philippines. She and her husband, Dennis, served as missionaries in Spain for twenty years, where they raised two daughters. Dennis and Nanette also ministered in music together for thirty-five years. Dennis's lifelong Type 1 diabetes combined with an abrupt diagnosis of brain cancer changed their lives overnight. Whether through other languages, music, or written words, Nanette has always been compelled to express what God has taught her and done in her life. She is presently training to become a hospital chaplain, enjoying the challenge of learning new ways to communicate God's love.

LET GOD'S UNFAILING LOVE
QUIET YOUR HEART

Lamentations 3:21–23 (NLT): Yet I still dare to hope when I remember this: the unfailing love of the Lord never ends! By his mercies we have been kept from complete destruction. Great is his faithfulness; his mercies begin afresh each day.

A Season of Sorrows, A Season of Hope

For years I dreamed of becoming a counselor, one who could help people heal from traumatic memories, who could encourage them with God's unfailing love and hope. I did not know the journey would involve healing from new memories of my own.

Years of working with students and women helped me prepare to help others. But I didn't begin graduate school until I was a grandmother, joking that I hoped to finish my studies before I needed a walker to get to work. My husband patiently supported me through long hours of studying, writing papers, and going to class. It seemed like everything was on track.

Midway through graduate school, a friend's betrayal brought unimaginable sorrow and unanswerable questions. A wise pastor encouraged me in the forgiveness process, helping me conceptualize what needed to be done anytime the painful situation came back to my mind: take her off my "hook" and put her on God's "hook." He helped me understand what the Bible describes as sharing the sufferings of Christ (1 Peter 4:13), encouraging me that God would use this pain to prepare me for serving Him in new ways. "I see you have forgiven her," he said. "But there is one more thing you need to do." "Yes, anything," I said, wanting to do all God required of me. "You need to pray God will bless her," he said.

I left his office, wondering how such behavior could be blessed. But I began to pray, "God, bless her," realizing this was not merely a pastor's suggestion but a biblical directive. And as I obeyed, I was freed from the anguish of that situation—God's mercies were enough for each day!

Immediate new challenges occurred as my father-in-law's health deteriorated with the ravages of Alzheimer's disease. At the same time, our oldest daughter, mother of two children, began to lose the ability to walk, her complex health concerns baffling the experts. God's unfailing love quieted our hearts. Daily we learned to hope in God, not our circumstances.

The season of difficulties continued when our youngest daughter gave birth to a son who was rushed to the Neonatal Intensive Care Unit (NICU) of a San Francisco hospital. I remember little about my hurried flight to San Francisco. I do remember checking into a hotel, clasping the tiny hands of four-year-old Mimi and one-year-old Maude, the two precious granddaughters who stayed with me there. I remember walking with our daughter and son-in-law into the NICU to meet this beloved newborn grandson.

His parents named him "Happy," and he looked perfect. But thick dark hair, chubby arms, ten fingers and ten toes could not offset catastrophic damage to his heart, lungs, and gastrointestinal system that would require five major surgeries in his first weeks of life. His body too fragile to move; I could not hold him. But I told him "I love you" and found skin to touch between myriad wires covering his tiny body. While machines blared dire messages and nurses checked monitors, people around the world were praying for this beloved boy.

From early in her pregnancy, our daughter and her husband had been told their son's development posed serious medical concerns. His heart wasn't developing normally; his lungs would likely be compromised. By the fifth month of her pregnancy, our daughter began receiving calls from a geneticist after each checkup, urging her to abort her son. She quit answering the phone after doctor visits.

At the NICU, I held my granddaughters up to see their brother and watched their love splash over him. After visiting hours, Mimi and Maude went with me to the hotel while their parents tried to rest at the Ronald McDonald House near the hospital. We had tea parties; we played with dolls; we hugged and read stories. Their laughter reminded me "the unfailing love of the Lord never ends!" It reminded me to trust God, not my agonized emotions.

The next day at the hospital, I was with Happy while his parents spent time with their daughters. I prayed and gently touched him, sang softly, and whispered "I love you," tears flowing unchecked. Glancing up, I was startled to see a NICU staff member studying me. She said, "Usually in, uh, cases like this, doctors advise parents to terminate the fetus. Do you know if your daughter was given that recommendation?"

Taking a moment to recover from the blunt force of her words, I prayed before speaking. "My daughter and son-in-law believe God creates each life; we believe their son's life has infinite value," I said. After looking at me with disdain, she abruptly left the room.

When his parents and sisters returned, Happy made his own statement about the significance of life. Hearing his parents' voices, his mouth set in determination, he turned his body toward them. Alarms sounded, and a nurse rushed to adjust his pain medication.

A few short weeks later, my husband and I returned to California, this time for our grandson's memorial service. His brief life mattered. God accomplished His perfect purpose through this precious one created in His image.

You, too, are created in God's image; your life matters to Him. Today you can hope, remembering: "the unfailing love of the Lord never ends! By his mercies we have been kept from complete destruction. Great is his faithfulness; his mercies begin afresh each day."

MARTI WIBBELS is a licensed mental health counselor and an International Board Certified Professional Christian Counselor who works at a counseling center in Boca Raton, Florida. She is the author of the novel *Secrets Behind the Door* and of a Bible study workbook, *The Art of Divine Contentment*. She and her husband, Alan, also coauthored a workbook for singles, *Relationships Pure and Simple*. Marti is mother of three daughters and grandmother of nine. Her web address: www.loringgate.com; e-mail: marti@loringgate.com.

WE CAN BE CONFIDENT
THAT HE WORKS ALL THINGS
TOGETHER FOR GOOD

Romans 8:28–29 (NASB): And we know that God causes
all things to work together for good to those who
love God, to those who are called according to His purpose.
For those whom He foreknew, He also predestined to become
conformed to the image of His Son, so that He would
be the firstborn among many brethren.

My Good and His Glory

 I was raised in a Christian home and gave my life to God at an early age. After graduating from Bible college, I taught mathematics for a year in an international Christian school in Seoul, South Korea. While there, I developed type-1, insulin-dependent diabetes. It was months before I realized what was going on and another year before I regained my health. When I returned home from Korea, I was twenty-five years old, living with my parents, and trying to regulate my blood sugars—not where I had planned my life to be at that point.

Diabetes is a great affliction for a legalist. If you enjoy self-regulation and checklists, this is the disease to have. Good diabetics measure everything they eat, eat at set times of the day, and exercise consistently. However, I am notoriously undisciplined, so this disease has not been easy for me. On one particularly hard day, I thought I had done everything right—I had exercised, carefully measured what I ate, and taken the right amount of insulin. But when I checked my blood sugar that evening, it was dangerously high. I was devastated—it was so hard for me to get it all right, and even my best efforts had miserably failed.

I grew up thinking that sickness was God's judgment on me. Now, I thought back on all the ways I had failed God during that day. According to my way of thinking, I of course deserved for my blood sugar to be out of whack! Wracked by self-condemnation, I managed to crawl over to my one-year Bible (which actually took me three years to read) and found the reading for that day. I wasn't searching for Scripture to make me feel better—this was the scheduled reading for that day. It was John 9 and began,

As he (Jesus) passed by, he saw a man blind from birth. And his disciples asked him, "Rabbi, who sinned, this man or his parents, that he was born blind?" Jesus answered, "It was not that this man sinned, or his parents, but that the works of God might be displayed in him."

Then Jesus healed the man, giving further evidence to the onlookers of His power as God.

I sobbed as I read this. In that moment, I came to understand something about my diabetes, and more importantly, something about God's Word. I realized my diabetes wasn't God's judgment on me. Upon further study, I came to understand that Christ bore all of God's judgment against me when He died on the cross, and there is now no condemnation on those who are in Jesus (Romans 8:1). God has allowed me to bear the burden of diabetes for my good and His glory. And I can testify twelve years later that this has truly been the case. From that day on, I *never* again saw my diabetes as judgment from God. Instead, it was an avenue to bring Him glory. This was a radical change to my thinking.

Even more important, in that night of Bible reading, I began to understand something I had heard from others for years but didn't really appreciate for myself—that God speaks through His Word in a very real, personal way. His Word is supernatural and living. It's alive! I don't know how to explain it. But I've experienced it enough to believe it's true. The Bible isn't simply a collection of important stories about

God. It's a living book that supernaturally speaks to us today. The Spirit uses this book in an incredible way to meet us in our personal, twenty-first-century needs.

But this requires that we *open the Book*. I praise God that twelve years ago, on a night when I was devastated by Satan's lies to me about my illness, God moved me to open His Book and then spoke to me in a real way that has sustained and encouraged me with every diabetic battle I've faced since then. I haven't opened the Book every day since then as I should. And God hasn't always spoken to me as clearly as He did that night. But He's shown me a lot of Himself in ways that make me thirst for more of Him. It's this thirst that draws me back to the Word time after time.

WENDY ALSUP is a wife and mom living in Seattle, Washington. She teaches math at a local community college and is the author of *Practical Theology for Women: How Knowing God Makes a Difference in Our Daily Lives.* theologyforwomen.blogspot. com

If you need Him, that's where He is. The Word.

"For the word of God is living and active, sharper than any two-edged sword, piercing to the division of soul and of spirit, of joints and of marrow, and discerning the thoughts and intentions of the heart" (Hebrews 4:12).

HE WILL RENEW US DAY BY DAY

2 Corinthians 4:16 (NIV): Therefore we do not lose heart.
Though outwardly we are wasting away, yet inwardly
we are being renewed day by day.

Miracles and Healing

 "How did you meet your husband?" an acquaintance asked.

While sometimes I just reply, "at church," I sensed the Holy Spirit nudging me to give the longer version.

"Actually . . . I was dating his brother."

"Oooh! This sounds like a good story. Let's hear it!" she says.

"It is a good story . . . I was dating T.J.'s brother, Chris, when he died of cancer."

Usually at this point, the person asking feels terrible and doesn't know how to respond. It's then when I have the opportunity to share God's faithfulness through Chris's death.

Chris and I started dating in May of 1998. He was twenty-six, and I was twenty-four. Chris was in remission from cancer. He was coming out of a year and a half of three major surgeries, chemotherapy, and radiation. With an initially grim prognosis, he appeared to be in remission and on the road to full recovery. He had a new lease on life and was excited to serve God.

We dated through the summer and I got to know his best friends, his family, and his life. We had similar personalities—enthusiastic, impulsive, adventurous—and were beginning to fall in love.

In September of 1998, Chris walked into the classroom where I taught fourth grade. He had just returned from an oncology checkup and his face told me what I didn't want to hear. The sarcoma in his spine had returned and was rapidly moving up his spinal column, soon to be in his brain. There were no treatment options.

That night I was invited to dinner with his family. Before dinner I had a little time alone. I opened my Bible and begged God to show me hope. I prayed, "Lord, You are the God of miracles. Please show us a miracle."

From day one of his cancer returning, each and every one of us closest to Chris prayed for a radical miracle. As Chris became sicker and weaker, he moved back into his parents' house. Every night we read the Bible at his bedside and asked God to heal him. And every day I saw miracles take place. They weren't the miracles I had hoped for, but looking back, I clearly see them as miracles.

Chris was a faithful soldier. His spiritual strength and fervor were miracles. He accepted that he would soon be in heaven. He admitted he was scared but had great peace and confidence—helping the rest of us deal with his illness. He exemplified 2 Corinthians 4:16: "Therefore we do not lose heart. Though outwardly we are wasting away, yet inwardly we are being renewed day by day."

I experienced miracles in my life as God daily provided exactly what I needed to get through the anguish of the situation. I never had anyone close to me die before. I was terrified of death, of spiraling into depression after he was gone, of not being able to cope with it all. I confided these fears to my loving mentor. She said if I focus on my fears—and what may or may not happen in the days ahead—I will spiral out of control. But if I stay with the Lord, in today, He will provide exactly what I need. I found this to be true as I traveled the journey with Chris.

I remember sharing with Chris that I would never find another man of his caliber. He replied, "You will. Just promise me you won't compromise."

Chris went home to be with Jesus on December 20, 1998. We had prayed for a miraculous healing every day—even up to the moment he died. He received the ultimate healing in heaven where he no longer had to suffer in his physical body. I experienced healing by depending on God for every bit of strength. He didn't let me fall apart.

I stayed close with Chris's family in the months and years to come. T.J. and I became great friends and started spending more time together. We gradually fell in love. We got married in November of 2001. Chris had thought the world of his older brother, T.J., and would be thrilled to know I didn't compromise. T.J. and I would never know each other in the way we do now had we not walked through Chris's death together. We have sweet memories of Chris and still talk about him. We also laugh because Chris and I were too similar to get married—we would've driven each other nuts.

Chris fulfilled what God had for him here on earth. He taught us how to live, and he taught us how to die. Chris lived this: "For to me, to live is Christ and to die is gain" (Philippians 1:21).

DANIELLE E. CROWELL lives in Metamora, Illinois, with her husband, T.J. She has been published in *I'm Glad I'm a Mom* by Hearts at Home, and Focus on the Family's *Focus on Your Child* magazine. Danielle taught school for seven years before becoming a stay-at-home mom with their children Grace, Caroline, and Jeremiah.

REST IN THE SAFETY OF YOUR
HEAVENLY FATHER'S ARMS

Exodus 15:2 (NIV): The Lord is my strength and my song;
he has become my salvation. He is my God, and I will praise him,
my father's God, and I will exalt him.

Abba, Our Father

 Tucked away among my treasury of favorite childhood memories is a vivid mental image of one of those rare evenings when my dad would come in from the field and declare that we were all going for a drive right after supper. Throughout the meal, the excitement would build until finally the dishes were done and we would all clamber into our old station wagon, loudly calling dibs for the prize spot between Daddy and Mother in the front seat, or second best—one of the backseat windows. There was something wonderful about having our whole family tucked safely and snugly into that car.

Daddy would turn out of the driveway and start down the dusty country roads at a leisurely pace, slowing even more to check a field of ripening wheat or a fence that needed mending. Sometimes we had to wait quietly, but oh so impatiently while he stopped in the middle of the road to visit with a fellow farmer who was out checking his own crops.

Our drives inevitably took us into town. We wouldn't dare say anything, but all of us kids would be peeking out the window hoping and praying that Daddy would turn the car in the direction of the local Dairy Queen. Sometimes he purposely took the long way around, pretending to head back home, then laughing when our obvious disappointment turned to joy as he steered again in the direction of ice cream.

My favorite part of those evenings was playing 'possum in the backseat of the car, in the hopes that when we got home, he would carry me into the house and tuck me into bed. There was no warmer, safer feeling than being held in my father's big, strong arms.

Those happy memories will always remind me that I am safe in the arms of God. I am so thankful for the strength and security and love my dad provided as an earthly father, so now that I'm a grown-up woman with children of my own, I can understand the strength and security of my *heavenly* Father.

It breaks my heart to think of the woman who was abandoned or who never knew the love of a father; or worse, whose earthly father harmed her in ways that cause her to now fear even the idea of a Father God. But the Bible tells us in Deuteronomy 10:18 that God has promised to defend the cause of the fatherless. All through the Scriptures God is portrayed as a loving, kind, just Father to each of His children, but especially to those who don't have an earthly father.

How blessed we are that God is a redeemer, not only of our souls, but of our broken hearts and dreams. We have the precious privilege of coming before the God of the universe, calling Him *Abba*, Daddy, and knowing that He will scoop us up into the safety of His loving arms.

DEBORAH RANEY is at work on her seventeenth novel. Her books have won the RITA Award, the HOLT Medallion, the National Readers' Choice Award, and the Silver Angel from Excellence in Media. Deborah's first novel, *A Vow to Cherish*, inspired the World Wide Pictures film of the same title. Deb also serves on the advisory board of American Christian Fiction Writers. She and her husband, Ken, have four children and enjoy small-town life in Kansas. Visit her website at www.deborahraney.com.

GOD IS GRACIOUS ENOUGH TO WELCOME
OUR HONEST SORROWS AND OUR DEEPEST LONGINGS,
AS WELL AS OUR JOYS AND OUR PRAISE

Psalm 55:6 (KJV): And I said, "Oh that I had wings like a dove!
For then would I fly away, and be at rest."

"On This Day"

I remember November 30, 1988. On this day, I awoke, ecstatic. I was practicing lines of the Christmas program in my head, eager for the program that we students in the mission school were giving that evening for our families.

It had been three months now since I last saw my family, when I boarded the little Cessna on the grass strip of our African village and waved good-bye on the boarding stairs, then again out the window as we sped along the airstrip and lifted off.

The time since then had passed quickly. I had also turned nine the previous month, and knew my family would now celebrate my birthday and my brother's fourth birthday together, as soon as we made it back home. My dad had acquired our first car, so they decided to make the road trip instead of having my sister Helen and me fly home as we had always done before. I knew they were now loaded up in the Isuzu beginning the drive that would bring them along many lonely dirt roads, winding through villages and across open plains, to arrive here.

We would perform for the families tonight!

So that afternoon, we students filed out the drive-up area to await the arrivals. As each vehicle arrived, I craned my neck to see my mom's long arm waving out the window and my brother Alex's goofy grin peering out from her lap.

But other cars came, parents claimed their clamoring kids, and my family had not appeared. Finally, a lady I recognized as the mom of some friends who lived fairly near us said something to our dorm mother, gesturing in our direction. She then came and told us to go ahead and get ready for the program.

I was disappointed, but assumed my family would arrive at any moment. My mental image just altered itself to adjust to a late clamor of hugs and kisses rushed in before the program started . . . but the program began and ended, and still they had not arrived.

The next morning we were taken to the Cessna, and told we were going to go back to our village by air after all. This time I imagined the whole family standing there on the airstrip, coming into focus as the plane landed, with eager smiles and waves—still, no. The parents of a classmate took us in their car instead—so of course I changed my expectation once more, this time thinking they were taking us to our house where the family would be waiting in front of our little home.

Instead we arrived at our classmate's house. Auntie Elaine (all family friends were "Auntie" and "Uncle" to us kids) asked Helen and me to come and sit with her on the couch.

"Anna, Helen—I have some really sad news . . . there was a car accident . . . your daddy went to heaven . . ." Before the sentence was finished, I had burst into loud sobs. Helen looked at me and started crying, and Auntie Elaine and her daughter were both crying and hugging us.

I barely remember any mention of the rest of the family at that point. The rest of the day and many days after that passed in a sort of a fog.

I remember falling asleep, dreaming fitfully, waking up convinced the whole awful thing was only a nightmare and that Daddy would walk in and comfort me.

I can remember being reunited with my brothers, who had been injured in the accident. I would stare at Alex's discolored and misshapen head and cart Ian around carefully in his body cast.

I remember visiting Mom there in the Zambian hospital, horrified at the sight of my strong, active, beautiful mother lying there on the stretcher bed unable to move herself. I hated seeing Mom like that and dreaded the visits, and I hated myself for feeling that way, thinking there must be something wrong with me if I didn't want to see my mother.

Somehow, time passed. My daddy's funeral passed in a blur of friends, strangers, languages I didn't know, and wails I knew only too well. As soon as Mom was strong enough to be transported, we were shipped to the U.S., where hospitalization and then physical rehab awaited her. I took refuge in my books, in beautiful worlds of fantasy, to the extent that my grandmother still teases me for always having my "nose stuck in a book" as a child.

And eventually Mom was well enough to take care of the four of us again. I still don't know for the life of me how she—now a paraplegic—did it, supporting and caring for a home of her own and four children. She did it well . . . she loved us well.

On this day, when I was a child, Mom beautifully commemorated the anniversary of the accident. She would buy what seemed like hundreds of helium-filled balloons, bringing them home so they filled the house. Then she tied note cards to the string of each one, and told us to write on them—as many as we wanted, and whatever we wanted to say. I remember writing things like "Jesus loves me this I know" and "My daddy died on this day, and he is now in heaven with God, because he loved God. I do too." I wrote silly notes, but meaningful ones, longing, in all my childhood intensity, to somehow tell the world that I had a great daddy, and that someday I would see him again.

Since her family returned to the U.S. from the mission field, Anna spent her childhood and early adulthood traveling throughout the world, thanks to mission and work opportunities. Her undergraduate degree in French literature led to a master's degree in information sciences. She has worked as a college and high school librarian, cross country coach, youth leader, and a homeschooling teacher. This year she will return to Zambia to teach grades 1 and 2 for a British boarding school, all the while continuing pursuing her passions of writing, artwork, photography, and running.

HE BRINGS BEAUTY OUT OF ASHES

John 15:1–2 (NIV): I am the true vine, and my Father is the gardener.
He cuts off every branch in me that bears no fruit, while every branch
that does bear fruit he prunes so that it will be even more fruitful.

A Birth and a ReBirth

 Eight years ago I became a mom, but it wasn't my first pregnancy. I had lost a baby to a miscarriage, and I'd had an abortion eleven years before that. My daughter's birth was a sort of rebirth for me and so I celebrate this day with her. She is nothing less than a gift from the Lord.

I had spent the years prior to her birth aching because of my poor judgment in choosing to abort my first pregnancy. I spun in a cycle of shame, deceit, denial, and fear. I built a wall up around me to ensure my shameful secret would not be discovered. I spent years in denial, pushing what I had done back to the recesses of my mind. And I was afraid of being found out, being thought a hypocrite, and worst of all—fearful that I would never have the chance for another baby.

I couldn't forgive myself. But I learned that God could.

When I became pregnant in early 1999, ten years to the month after I had become pregnant before, I felt redeemed. Restored. Forgiven. I felt that the Lord had smiled at me and told me it was okay and that He loved me. Surely, this was my rainbow—my promise that all was forgiven! But when an ultrasound later revealed that there was no heartbeat, I felt that my own heart had been shattered, again, at that very moment.

What had happened to the love and forgiveness that the Lord had bestowed on me just a few short weeks earlier?

Despair covered me and seeped through me. I felt abandoned by Him, and fell into a dark, deep pit. All of the years I had spent trying to cover it up and hiding from it came crashing down upon me.

That pregnancy had signified so much in my mind. The miscarriage signified even more.

I cried out to Him and fell on my knees and searched His Word—looking for answers. Looking for Him. Asking Him, why?

From that despair, I was led to a Bible study for women healing from abortions, and through that study, He met with me. I found Him and He began to heal me from the shame, and from the fear of my sin being discovered. He tore down the wall I had built around myself, and surrounded me with His mercy.

He showed me, through His Word, that His love for me was the same as it had always been. My feelings had not changed His. Who He is and the truth of that were not dependent on what I thought. He is the Alpha and the Omega and my actions were not too great for Him to forgive. His Word was a healing balm to my soul, a steady quenching rainfall on dry soil. All of the years of suffering and basing the Lord's forgiveness on my circumstances . . . when all along, I had been forgiven. He had been waiting for me to reach out and take His outstretched hand.

A year later, to the month, I was pregnant again. This time, it was different. This time, I got it: He had never stopped loving me. He had restored me and I would never be the same.

When I held my daughter for the first time, and as I fell deeply in love with her, I understood, in a very small way, the powerful transforming love that He has for me and for all of His children. A love so great and deep that He would stop at nothing to reveal it to me.

Once again, the Lord had sent a small babe into the world to bring hope and restoration.

KARLA PORTER is a wife, mama, writer, speaker, and designer. Her current exercise regimen consists mainly of attempting to scale Mount Laundry, though she hopes to run her first marathon soon. You can find her online blogging about her crazy life at *Looking Towards Heaven* http://karlascrazylife.blogspot .com), and as founder of ModernMediaMom.com.

GOD SEES YOU THROUGH

*Isaiah 26:3 (KJV): Thou will keep him
in perfect peace, whose mind is stayed on thee:
because he trusteth in thee.*

Look Backward for Forward Faith

 Several years after I became a wife and mother, I found myself in a season in which I allowed the burden of my to-do lists to overwhelm me. I couldn't get everything done. I was at the end of my rope and almost in a semidepression. I felt like a world-class swimmer forgetting how to swim in the middle of a race and having to dog-paddle instead.

But there had been a time in my life when things were much simpler and purer in my walk with Christ. I started to remember what it was like when I was young.

When you grow up in a pastor's family, you digest the Word of God right along with the baby food. Some of my earliest memories are of the beginning days of our church when we only had a few people. I didn't mind. I loved hearing preaching even as a child. At that time it wasn't because the words, or the doctrines—more the ebb and flow of my dad's voice. He used his voice not only to preach in the pulpit but also to praise me, to tell me that he loved me and that he was proud of me. Mom did the same thing.

As an adult, I see the idyllic world of my childhood in a different light, making me admire my parents even more. These were people who rented a small storefront Sunday after Sunday hoping and praying that someone would be at the service. They were two young people fresh out of college from small towns in Kentucky and Ohio, trying to make it in the big city on 3200 West Fullerton Avenue in Chicago. They persevered even though the church wasn't paying them a salary and they both had to find jobs to make a living wage in addition to getting the church off the ground. This wasn't fun and games with two kids in diapers and many adjustments to be made.

Now I was the one with kids and in a busy point in my own life. I found that I'd gotten off the path of my spiritual journey. I'd started substituting the things I did for Him for closeness with Him . . . it was easier to *do* than to *be*.

In Jerusalem last year, our tour group stayed in the same hotel as Beth Moore, the well-known Bible teacher and author. I really wanted to meet her but I was shy. I didn't want to go up to her and talk since I was sure that hundreds of other people did that daily. She breakfasted in the same room as our group, so Neal, my husband, came and got me and said he wanted to introduce me to her and get our picture taken together.

Our nine-year-old daughter, Amanda, traveled with us too. She came up to me wanting to talk. Neal took my arm. "We need to go talk to Beth now," he said.

Amanda took hold of my hand. "No, Mom. *We* need to talk. Now."

I looked at Neal. I looked at Amanda. Her eyes filled with a pleading no mother could ignore. "I have to go talk with Amanda," I said.

My daughter and I went off to a corner.

"I've had some doubts about my salvation. I'm worried I'm not really saved," Amanda said.

When I was eight, I sat by my dad, summoning the courage to ask him the same question. I've never forgotten Dad's answer—in fact I still think of it when I have doubts today.

"That's just the Devil trying to make you doubt, Julie," he said. "When that happens just repeat John 3:16 over and over until the doubts go away."

So in classic déjà vu, I said the same thing to my own daughter.

God loved her. And the truth became startlingly clear to me. God loved me.

He sent His Son for Amanda. He sent His Son for me.

If Amanda believed, she wouldn't perish. If I believed, I wouldn't perish. Amanda could have everlasting life.

Belief wasn't about doing. I'd learned this truth at four and accepted Jesus. But then I had to discover it anew when it came to the daily cares of a busy life. It wasn't about works. It was about faith. Somehow I'd lost sight of this simplest of simple truths.

I've tried to keep this truth close to my heart when I'm tempted to think again that it's all about doing.

JULIE SCUDDER DEARYAN has edited *Victory In Grace* magazine for thirteen years. *Victory In Grace* is a TV and radio ministry dedicated to helping people find victory through God's amazing grace. She is excited about passing on a heritage of faith to her two children.

ANSWERED PRAYERS ARE
THE FATHER'S PEARLS

Hebrews 13:5 (NLT): Don't love money;
be satisfied with what you have. For God has said,
"I will never fail you. I will never abandon you."

Everyday Pearls

 "God, how can You use me today?" You might be asking that very question.

Some of the women writing for this book have experienced grinding trials. And you know what? God is using them today!

But perhaps some of you reading these stories can't relate entirely to these types of trials. Your life is filled with puppy messes on the carpet, washer hose explosions, hubby's flu (the same time as yours), and physical challenges (too much weight, not enough exercise). That's day-to-day reality for many of us. So what and where are our pearls?

As the first part of Matthew 13:44 says, "The Kingdom of Heaven is like a treasure that a man discovered hidden in a field." *Hidden.* Most of the time our pearls are hidden from sight because they're small and easily left unnoticed.

If you look at my life, there are jillions of pearls! By some standards, my favorite pearl was pretty tiny, but I've remembered it for over thirty years. God had brought me through some grinding times of spiritual questioning, job searching, and family disagreements. As a result, the door was opened to attend mission school (New Tribes Bible Institute).

One time as I walked to my part-time job, my feet were cold that frigid, Wisconsin winter afternoon. I grumbled a complaint to God, yet He received it as a prayer. Because, when I returned to the dorm, my mailbox contained a warm pair of socks left anonymously. That "pearl" felt mighty good on my next walk. Answered prayers are the beautiful pearls left by my heavenly Abba Father after grinding experiences.

Don't miss the pearls . . . no matter what size . . . that God has given you.

CHRIS SHENK says, "For all of my years a sovereign God has walked with me through life. On the other hand, I've walked with Him for fewer years than He's been with me! However, He has brought me to the place where I'm useful to Him through producing a daily radio program with Campus Crusade for Christ. God has blessed me with Steve, a godly husband of over twenty-five years."

Get Connected!

Thank you, dear reader, for making a difference in the lives of others. You are cordially invited to become one of the PEARL GIRLS™. Please visit www.pearlgirls.info and click on Post-a-Pearl. Share your story of encountering grit and experiencing grace and read the many other stories that are posted. Get connected.

Any funds that I receive from this book will go in full to WINGS (Women in Need Growing Stronger) and Hands of Hope. WINGS (www.wingsprogram.com) provides shelter in a safe house for women and children fleeing from domestic violence in the northwest Chicago suburbs and helps them get a second start in life through transitional homes and programs. Hands of Hope (www.handsofhopeonline.com) helps build wells in African villages.

A Word of Thanks

I would like to thank the many wonderful women who "tithed their talent" by writing essays for this special project. Thank you for sharing your gift.

And thank you to the incredible editors and to the sales team at Moody Publishers. It has been an honor to launch PEARL GIRLS™ with you.

Thanks to my extraordinary agent, Janet Kobobel Grant, founder of Books & Such Literary Agency. Her wisdom and friendship are true treasures.

Thank you to Amy Lathrop, a dear friend, whose patience and attention to detail are unrivaled.

A final thank-you to my beloved husband, David McSweeney, who has supported this project from the start, along with my daughters, Melissa and Katie. You are such blessings in my life!

Let's close this part of our journey with a benediction:

"The Lord bless you and keep you; the Lord make His face shine upon you and be gracious to you; the Lord turn His face toward you and give you peace" (Numbers 6:24–26).

God bless!

Margaret McSweeney
www.pearlgirls.info

MEET ME AT THE WELL

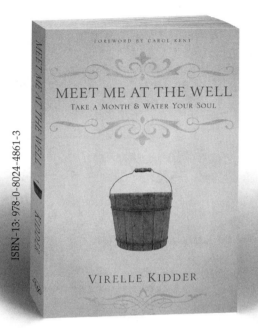

MOODY
PUBLISHERS.

1-800-678-8812 · MOODYPUBLISHERS.COM

THE UNCOMMON WOMAN

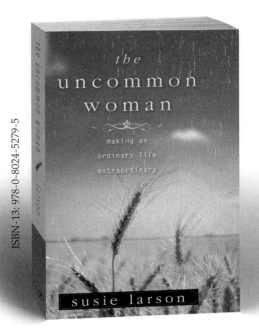

This book is for the woman who longs to rise up out of the stereotypical behavior of gossip, insecurity, pettiness, and small dreams. She has an unfulfilled desire to be someone who goes against the grain of the common for the sole purpose of living a life with conviction. The woman who reads this book is ready to believe in her deep value, ready to accept her high calling, and ready to make a difference in a world in need of her influence.

Find out more about author Susie Larson by visiting:
www.susielarson.com | susielarsonblog.typepad.com

MOODY
PUBLISHERS.

1-800-678-8812 · MOODYPUBLISHERS.COM

DAILY SEEDS